Leckie×Leckie

Scotland's leading educational publishers

CfE Higher

RELIGIOUS, MORAL & PHILOSOPHICAL STUDIES

GRADE A BOOSTER

D1513721

David Jack

CfE Higher RELIGIOUS, MORAL & PHILOSOPHICAL STUDIES GRADE A BOOSTER

© 2015 Leckie & Leckie Ltd

001/10062015

10 9 8 7 6 5 4 3 2

ISBN 9780007590902

Published by
Leckie & Leckie Ltd
An imprint of HarperCollins*Publishers*
Westerhill Road, Bishopbriggs, Glasgow, G64 2QT
T: 0844 576 8126   F: 0844 576 8131
leckieandleckie@harpercollins.co.uk
www.leckieandleckie.co.uk

Publisher: Katherine Wilkinson
Project manager: Keren McGill & Craig Balfour

Special thanks to
Roda Morrison (copy edit)
Louise Robb (proofread)
Jouve (layout)
Ink Tank (cover)

Material taken from SQA documents reproduced with permission Copyright © Scottish Qualifications Authority.

Printed by CPI Group (UK) Ltd, Croydon, CR0 4YY

A CIP Catalogue record for this book is available from the British Library.

Contents

Basic stuff

How will this book help me?

This book is designed to help you get the best possible grade you can manage at Higher Religious, Moral and Philosophical Studies (RMPS from now on because I have no intention of writing that mouthful out every time I mention the exam!). It will explain the following:

- How the exam is set up
- How to write a decent assignment
- How to write a decent essay
- What kind of questions to expect in the exam.

Don't make the mistake, as some people do, of thinking that RMPS is an easy Higher. Many pupils get good marks in RMPS because they are in S6 and have a stack of Highers already, because the person teaching them is just the business and because many pupils put in that extra effort because it takes a bit of guts to do this Higher in the first place. Anybody who decides that they can wing it through this exam with the minimum of effort is going to be really disappointed when the envelope comes through the door in August.

How is the book organised?

This series is part of the Grade A Booster Series and as such its aim is to help people like you get a better grade. The exam is a written exam and, worse still, it is a written exam with essays. One of the biggest challenges you will have is putting together a decent essay which will usually be worth 10 or 20 marks. Be aware, however, that with the exam being new there might be changes to the marks range. Check with your teacher for the latest position. So what we have to do is find a way of helping you to put in writing what you say in those stormy discussions in your Higher RMPS class. All these brilliant ideas and contributions you make in class seem to disappear from your cranium the minute you are asked to put pen to paper.

This is how I have set things out:

- The majority of the topics have been covered in this book. However, if you have studied one of the topics that are not in this book, I have not left you out! You can find free-to-download chapters for these topics on the Free Resources page of the Leckie & Leckie website at: www.leckieandleckie.co.uk/page/Resources.
- Chapter 2 is on the assignment.

- Chapter 3 explains how the exam works.
- Chapter 4 tells you how to write essays.
- The remaining chapters pick out the most obvious areas for each topic in each unit. It's not possible to cover them all so it might well be that some areas come up that are not in this book; in which case ... nae luck!
- In these chapters there are also examples of the kinds of statements that might precede questions – these will help you to get used to the wording and get over your fears of these statements, many of which are not nearly as complicated or sophisticated as they look.

How should I use this book?

There are a few different ways you can use this book:

- You can leave it open on your desk to pretend that you really have been studying and not playing your Xbox or sticking scraps in your scrapbook. Be sure to highlight lines in the book and dog-ear the page corners though. Coffee cup rings on random pages are an excellent ploy.
- You can produce it in your RMPS class and tell the teacher that you would recommend this excellent book for the entire class and that they should all buy one for themselves and one for their parents.
- You can dip in and out of it according to the problems you are encountering in your answering techniques and then apply the suggestions to the next past paper or homework task you do.

Before you start

You need two things before you start to read this book and both are on the SQA website:

- A copy of the SQA Arrangements for the units and options you're doing.
- A copy of the Specimen Question Paper and Past Papers.

You may need to refer to these as we go along. Check that your teacher has referred to them recently too because things do change in the documentation. A friendly 'Haw you, aye ... you! You checked the SQA arrangements recently by the way?' is the default way to address teachers, and you will find that most teachers respond to this with a cheery demeanour.

The exam structure

The assignment

Your teacher will explain the arrangements for the assignment. Furthermore he/she/it will tell you about it in September and say that the plan is to do the assignment in December. This probably won't happen because seven of the class will be involved in carol concert rehearsals, three in organising the senior Christmas dance, four of you taking Christmas hampers to pensioners and two of you will have an extra shift at Primark. It might be a rush job a week before the due date so be ready for it. More advice later.

The exam

This lasts for a colossal two hours and fifteen minutes after which you leave the school and head for the nearest casualty department who will use specialist equipment to get your hand out of the 'pen grasp' in which it has become locked.

Be warned folks, Higher RMPS is a pretty gruelling exam. It's over two hours long and that is a lot of writing and thinking. You really do need to be on top of your studying and on top of your game to do well in this exam.

CHAPTER 2

The assignment

Introduction

The assignment is probably the part of the course assessment that causes the most anxiety for staff and pupils (or practitioners and learners as they are now called by people who should know better). There are reasons for teachers feeling like this:

- Concern that you guys will faff about for months and end up doing a rush job
- Concern that you guys will under-perform and put a lot of pressure on yourselves in the exam.

For pupils there are concerns too:

- Concerns about what issue to do
- Concerns about whether or not you are doing it the right way
- Concerns about the write up.

So, in this chapter what we are going to do is help to remove these concerns and help you to get the best mark possible for the assignment. To do that you have to take the assignment seriously. You have to recognise that while the content of the exam is a mystery, the content of the assignment is not. Why would that be? It's because you choose the issue, you set the question, you can change the question and you know what you get marks for. It is understandable that you may not get the full 30 marks for the assignment because that is hard no matter who you are. However, you should be setting a goal of getting a minimum of 23/30 which is around 75%. That kind of mark can be gained through hard work alone. Seriously, it really can. Very often teachers find that those who don't put the effort into this kind of assessment have marks that reflect that.

The message is: do not mess about with this assessment. Get it done and get it done right.

Choosing the issue

The rules are that you can choose to do any issue you like and explore its significance and/or impact. This means that you do not have to do an issue from any of the units that you are studying. It can be on any religious, moral or philosophical issue. Can you do it on some obscure Buddhist belief held by the tribes of eastern Mongolia? You sure can. Can you do it on some bizarre moral issue like the morality of bee-keeping? Yup. Or what about a philosophical issue like the omniscience of RMPS teachers? Go for it!

On second thoughts, eh, no; don't do any of these issues. You need to be sensible about the issue you choose and the best thing to do is to choose an issue from the units you are doing and to make sure that it is directly related to something that might come up in the exam. What is the reasoning behind this?

- Issues you do in class will be in your notes so that saves you doing some research.
- Your teacher will be explaining the issues to you in some depth so that means that you will know a bit more about your issue rather than having to start from scratch.
- You may have done homework essays/assessments on the issue so that means you have a good idea of the standard you are writing at on the issue, and what you need to do to improve.
- There is a chance that your assignment issue will come up in the exam in which case it is your lucky day because you have done loads of work on it and can write a belter of an answer.
- There is a chance that in the exam some of the research you have done could be used to improve the quality of your response.

'But,' you cry, 'I thought CfE was about personalisation and choice; it is very disappointing to see you suggest that we don't go off on some flight of fancy.'

Get over yourself! Exams are about passing. What do you want to be able to say: 'I got an A in my RMPS Higher' or 'I failed my RMPS Higher but I exercised my right to personalisation and choice and did an assignment on the morality of keeping hamsters in captivity.' It is a no brainer – do not do a daft RMPS assignment issue.

So how do you choose an issue? You are expected to come up with suggestions yourself. This can be done in several ways:

- Browsing on the web and seeing what people are saying about your area of interest. The BBC religion and ethics pages are a good starting point.
- Going to the school library and looking at the extensive philosophy, religion and morality section while trying to eat your cheese straws without the librarian noticing.
- Going to your local library to browse through its extensive philosophy, religion and morality section and then asking the librarian where Libraria actually is and can you get a package holiday there.
- Contacting your local university library and asking if you can get access to its splendid resources so you can get half days off school and pretend you are researching rather than stuffing your face with muffins in some trendy coffee shop.
- Buying this book and choosing one of the titles listed below (so if you are browsing through this in Waterstones, either buy it or put it back, or if you have borrowed it from your pal please remember that your pal has almost certainly got some vile infection which is transmitted through paper).

Whatever you do, make sure that the issue you choose is an open question and not one that is closed, i.e. can be answered yes or no.

To help you on your way here are a few suggestions about the kind of thing you can do:

World Religion

I've gone for general titles here because these will give you an overview of the religion, and the research related to them will have a good chance of covering something that will come up in the exam. This unit is quite difficult to do an assignment on because there is a high risk that it could be very descriptive and not actually debate an issue. Take care to avoid that if you decide to do an assignment from this unit.

- To what extent are [choose your religion]'s festivals out of date?
- How important is [founder of your religion] in contemporary [your religion] thought?
- How important is it to understand [your religion] in the modern world?
- To what extent does [your religion] have a positive or negative impact on the world today?
- How far does the [sacred book of your religion] bring more good than evil to the world today?
- How far has [your religion] shaped the world we live in?

Morality and Belief

Many of you will choose this unit because many of the issues are out there and debated in the canteen or the late slip queue. Moral issues are probably the easiest ones to do because most of them are in the news and have NGOs (non-governmental organisations) working on the issues related to them:

Religion and Justice

- 'If the death penalty is effective in reducing crime, we need have no moral concerns.' How far do you agree? To what extent would executions be morally acceptable if they were humane?
- To what extent is it morally right for religions to condone execution?
- To what extent is our moral obligation to tackle the causes of crime greater than our moral obligation to punish the criminal?
- To what extent is it possible to justify punishment on moral grounds? Evaluate religious views on the death penalty.

Religion and Relationships

- To what extent should marriage be considered the norm for raising children?
- 'Pre-marital sex is morally acceptable.' Discuss the debate that might be raised by this statement.
- To what extent is it right for homosexuals to be allowed to marry?
- To what extent is feminism morally justifiable?
- How fair is it to suggest that religion is the cause of gender inequality?
- To what extent has religion been good for women?

Religion, Medicine and the Human Body

- To what extent is the sanctity of life a morally justifiable position?
- Which is more important: the rights of the embryo or scientific progress?
- To what extent might organ donation be considered unethical?
- To what extent should individuals have a duty to die rather than a right to die?
- Morally speaking, is palliative care any more moral than euthanasia?
- To what extent do doctors have more of a moral obligation to save lives than to act in a patient's best interests?

Religion and Global Issues

- To what extent is religious teaching to blame for environmental crises?
- To what extent is pollution a moral issue?
- How far do you agree that religion has nothing to contribute in the debate about stewardship? How far do rich countries have a moral obligation to help poor countries?
- To what extent are we morally obliged to give to charity?
- 'Giving aid can never be unethical.' To what extent is this statement true?

Religion and Conflict

- To what extent can wars be justified?
- To what extent can pacifism be justified?
- How far is the possession of a nuclear deterrent a moral issue?
- To what extent is UK foreign policy morally sound?
- To what extent can religious people support any war?
- 'The use of drones is morally unacceptable.' How far do you agree?

Religious and Philosophical Questions

In this unit there are four issues and there is much overlap between them so you might find that you are able to adapt the titles from one issue to another. You are allowed to do this mainly because you bought the book and it is your assignment. A word of warning about the issues here: some of the information you have to source uses highly technical language and it might take a few readings to understand it, so don't be discouraged.

Origins

- To what extent do you need both science and religion to explain the origins of life?
- To what extent do the discoveries of modern cosmology make it less likely that there is a God?
- To what extent would it be true to say that the theory of evolution has confirmed the existence of God?
- 'Scripture has nothing to offer in the debate about origins.' To what extent is this statement justifiable?

- 'The claim that God caused the universe is no more outrageous than the claim that it had a natural cause.' Discuss the validity of this statement.
- 'Evolution as the origins of life and God as the creator of life cannot both be right.' How strong are the claims surrounding this point of view?

The Existence of God

- To what extent is the cosmological argument stronger than the teleological argument?
- 'Science is all that is needed to disprove God's existence.' To what extent is this statement true?
- To what extent is it easier to defend the teleological argument than the cosmological argument?
- How sound is the argument that the existence of suffering and evil disproves the existence of God?
- To what extent is God's existence possible?
- How strong are the claims of atheism?

The Problem of Evil and Suffering

- To what extent are we free?
- How far do theodicies successfully explain suffering?
- To what extent does the existence of suffering and evil disprove the existence of God?
- 'All actions are pre-determined.' To what extent is this true?
- To what extent is the existence of evil illusory?
- 'Theodicies are excuses not explanations.' To what extent is this statement fair?

Miracles

- 'Miracles belong in the past, not the scientific age.' How far do you agree?
- To what extent are miracles possible?
- 'The laws of nature cannot be broken.' Discuss the debate that such a statement would create.
- 'Miracles only seem to be witnessed by believers.' How fair is this statement?
- To what extent are miracles necessary to prove the existence of God?
- 'If there are no miracles then there is no God.' How far is this view true?

What approach should I take?

The one approach you should **not** take is to embark on some long-winded descriptive piece of work. You could do a magnificent description and actually end up with very few marks. Best thing to do is to set a question for yourself and that way you will avoid producing a piece of description. The thing about asking yourself a question (like the ones listed above) is that you are not committed to that question. If you find that you have not really answered the question you set yourself you can adjust the question to suit what you have written.

What you are doing in RMPS is something that English teachers call a discursive essay. The discursive essay in English involves some research, note taking and planning the final piece of written work. The skills you use in RMPS are exactly the same as those you use in English. In fact, there might be some scope for using the same essay in both English and RMPS but you would need to discuss that with your teachers before taking a decision.

There are different types of discursive essay used in English which meet the requirements of the Higher RMPS assignment:

Argumentative

Argumentative writing will present an issue in such a way that a line of thought is developed dealing with two or more points of view, making clear the argument to be presented.

Persuasive

The aim of persuasive writing is to persuade the reader towards the writer's adopted point of view or purpose. It usually focuses on a single issue and it will carry a sense of conviction, commitment or belief through the conscious manipulation of language to create an appropriate tone.

Report

A report contains a number of key characteristics. It must contain information relevant to the chosen issue drawn from at least two sources and the material drawn from those sources must be recast and paraphrased appropriately according to the purpose of the report.

Your choice should depend on the approach with which you feel most comfortable. For example, if you find that you are scoring great marks in English for persuasive writing then that is the style you should opt for. Different people will obviously have different choices. The argumentative style will be chosen by those who have been suspended from school at least twice. The persuasive style will be chosen by those who sold their pet hamster to you as a very small Labrador pup and the report style will be chosen by those who did a sickeningly awesome report for their S1 RE project on Europe's Gothic cathedrals.

How is the assignment marked?

What they have in English is probably the most helpful way of gauging your performance. In English they do something called holistic marking which means that they read the whole piece of work looking for certain features and certain qualities rather than applying individual marks to each point that is made. This makes it sound a lot like markers having a gut feeling about the quality of your work and to an extent you are right but you find that if markers look at a batch of scripts and all have a go at saying what a script is worth there is very little, if any, difference in their views.

The SQA's marking instructions for the assignment have 'Top Secret' plastered all over them so these cannot be revealed here. You will probably find that your RMPS teacher is open to corruption and bribery and the offer of a year's supply of rolls and square sausage will be enough to make them squeal.

Now, I could go into demonstrating the skills in action but all that would do is make you panic. The trick is to write up your assignment in the same way as you would write your English discursive essay. Let the markers worry about the fine details of the assessment in your assignment report. The exemplars below cover all the skills you should have and deliberately do not go into how each one can be identified. Doing that would just create problems for you.

Knowledge and understanding

This is the factual stuff. You need to make sure that your facts are correct and relevant to the question you have set yourself. You also need to make sure that you have evidence that you have researched the issue and this can be done by making clear references to stuff you have researched. Try to have at least two pieces of evidence although you'll probably find that you look up more than two pieces.

Example of good knowledge and understanding
For some the most important issue in the debate about the treatment of embryos is women. One of the key issues in the embryo debate is abortion where the embryo is destroyed. The Abortion Rights organisation in the UK is quite clear about the impact of the law on women where they have to seek permission from doctors to get an abortion: 'This requirement is not only paternalistic, but more damagingly, it allows the approximately one in ten doctors who are opposed to all abortion the opportunity to delay, obstruct or even veto women's decisions.' This view is a comment on the UK law which seems to put the interests of the doctor and the embryo ahead of the woman.

A not-so-good example of knowledge and understanding
For some the treatment of embryos is a very important issue but not as important as women. The embryo gets destroyed in an abortion and some people think that it is okay to do that because women are more important in the debate. Women need to get their parents' permission to get an abortion and the permission of two GPs at their surgery.

Example of good analysis
Religious people therefore, on the whole, are uncomfortable with the idea of capital punishment. This stems from the various teachings they have on not killing. For Jews, the Ten Commandments make this demand and for Christians, Jesus, in each of the Gospels is quite clear that individuals should forgive their enemies and 'turn the other cheek' rather than going out to seek revenge. Both Hinduism and Buddhism have non-violence as a fundamental part of their morality. In Hinduism Gandhi's ahimsa demanded no violence, even in thought, towards another person.

Islam is often stereotyped as a religion that uses the death penalty indiscriminately but in fact the opposite is the case. There are states like Saudi Arabia and Iran who use it frequently but the reality is that it is not used as frequently as some suggest. On the other hand, the Qur'an says: 'Take not life, which God has made sacred, except by way of justice and law. Thus does He command you, so that you may learn wisdom.' However, compassion is strongly encouraged with the victim's family, in many cases, having the final say.

There is no doubt that religions consider life to be sacred and that their sacred books and traditions reinforce this. However, many of the sacred books were written against historical backgrounds where the death penalty was widely used even for quite trivial offences and support some use of the death penalty. The achievement of religions was to encourage a movement away from indiscriminate use of the death penalty, although it took centuries for that to happen. For those who interpret sacred books literally there can be no moving away from the truths contained in them so the death penalty remains a valid form of punishment. For those who see sacred books in their historical context the need to re-interpret these teachings on the death penalty and emphasise forgiveness is very great.

A not-so-good example of analysis

Religious people are very against capital punishment. The Ten Commandments say 'do not kill', and executing usually involves people dying a painful death like being electrocuted or given the lethal injection. Jesus said we should forgive our neighbours. Hindus and Buddhists are against all forms of violence and no Buddhist or Hindu countries have the death penalty.

Saudi Arabia and Iran use it frequently because the Qur'an says: 'Take not life, which God has made sacred, except by way of justice and law. Thus does He command you, so that you may learn wisdom.' This shows that Islam is the exception to the rule because it encourages its use.

Religions consider life to be sacred and therefore no religious person could ever be in favour of the death penalty because Jesus said that we should forgive our enemies.

A good example of evaluation

Most religious people would be uncomfortable with the legalisation of euthanasia. As already discussed this view is based on the idea that all life is sacred. The strength of such a view is that it means that everyone is protected and in particular those who are the most vulnerable in society. However, the problem with this view is that it fails to recognise that life sometimes loses its sacredness. Peter Suber argues, 'The chief difficulty with it is that it does not permit us to decide how to allocate our medical (and other) resources.' Suber is concerned that an absolute rule about the sanctity of life means that other considerations are overlooked. He goes on to say that in many cases people are just alive in the sense that a beetle is alive. We do not value the life of a beetle regardless of its condition, yet here we are saying that a human, who is no better condition, has a life that is sacred simply because they are human. The argument is attractive because it highlights the fact that humans pick and choose what qualifies as being sacred and, in the case of humans, it is no surprise that human life is sacred no matter what.

A not-so-good example of evaluation

Most religious people would be uncomfortable with the legalisation of euthanasia because life is sacred. The strength of such a view is that it means that everyone is protected. The view is *attractive because it highlights the fact that humans pick and choose what qualifies as being sacred so they always see human life in a favourable light. Therefore human life is not sacred.*

How much help can you get?

This is always an area of concern for staff, pupils and parents. There is always a fear that too much help is given and that this could be seen as cheating. The SQA clearly does not want teachers or kindly uncles to write the assignment for you. Nor do they want you to copy and paste stuff off Wikipedia and pretend it is your own. They want the work to be yours and they can tell whether it is or not.

You see, the people who mark the assignments are teachers and they know how a typical 16/17-year-old writes. They know the kind of vocabulary you work with and they know the kind of technical terms that most people of your age can handle. They can also spot a change of 'voice' in your writing. This happens when you write some of your own stuff and then copy and paste a bit from some academic website and pretend it is you. It sticks out like a sore thumb (although to be honest when my thumb is sore I tend to hold it under the opposite oxter rather than stick it out somewhere – but I digress). Also the websites and books you look at are often the same ones that markers will have looked at with their pupils or in their professional development activities (which makes them the great RMPS teachers that they are). In short, not much will get past markers. Google is a wonderful thing for checking out plagiarism and the SQA also has sophisticated software which can root out the plagiarists (who sound more like a religious cult than folk who copy stuff and pass it off as their own).

Teachers can help you. SQA says the help they are allowed to provide you with should be reasonable. While the teacher cannot sit over you, they can be on hand to give you advice and support in a professional manner ensuring that you are kept on the right track. Don't get hung up about this. If you need help, ask for it.

So that's the assignment. Probably the most important part of the exam because of the amount of control you have over it. You control the question, you control the content, you know where the marks are given. Everything you need to do well in an exam paper you haven't seen is sitting right in front of you in the assignment. Don't mess it up!

On the next page is the grid that is on the SQA website for the assignment marking:

A Researching the question or issue **C** Demonstrating knowledge and understanding of the question or issue

10-12	7-9	4-6	0-3
Evidence of: • consistently relevant knowledge points • consistently well-developed knowledge points • at least two sources **In response to the issue knowledge points are:** • skilfully selected • effectively deployed	**Evidence of** • mainly relevant knowledge points • mainly well-developed knowledge points • at least two sources **In response to the issue knowledge points are:** • mainly appropriate • generally well applied	**Evidence of:** • mainly relevant knowledge points • some developed knowledge points • at least one source **In response to the issue knowledge points are:** • mainly appropriate • inconsistently applied	Knowledge and sources are lacking and the candidate demonstrates little or no evidence of skill in this area.

B Analysing the question or issue **D** Synthesising information in a structured manner **E** Explaining the significance or impact of the question or issue in the contemporary world

8-10	6-7	4-5	0-3
Analysis will draw together a range of information and: • be sophisticated and consistently focused on the key issues • be present throughout the narrative • be evidenced by sources, observations, comments and arguments • clearly reflect the significance or impact of the issue	**Analysis be based on a range of information and:** • be straightforward and mainly focused on the key issues • be present at times in the narrative • be evidenced by sources, observations, comments or arguments at times • reflect the significance or impact of the issue	**Analysis will:** • be limited • be sporadic • have generally weak supporting evidence	Analysis is lacking and the candidate demonstrates little evidence of skill in this area. The assignment will be almost entirely descriptive.

F Evaluating different viewpoints on the question or issue, at least one of which must be religious **G** Presenting a reasoned and well-structured conclusion on the question or issue **H** Presenting a detailed explanation of supporting information and potential challenges or counter arguments

7-8	**Evaluation will include in depth judgements of the issue and:** • be sophisticated and consistently focused on the key issues • be present throughout the narrative • be consistently supported by evidence, exemplification or argument • **must** refer to a religious, moral or philosophical perspective • **must** include a clearly supported conclusion/ judgement on the issue • **must** include challenges/ counter arguments
5-6	**Evaluation will include judgements of the issue and:** • be straightforward and mainly focused on the key issues • be present at times in the narrative • be supported by evidence, exemplification or argument • **must** refer to a religious, moral or philosophical perspective • **must** include a supported conclusion/judgement on the issue • may include challenges/ counter arguments
3-4	**Evaluation will:** • be limited • be sporadic • have generally weak supporting evidence, exemplification or argument • refer to a religious, moral or philosophical perspective • include a conclusion/ judgement on the issue
0-2	Evaluation is lacking and the candidate demonstrates little evidence of skill in this area. The assignment will be almost entirely descriptive or analytical. Evaluative statements will tend to be of a simplistic and personal nature.

Exam game plan

What is being assessed?

The SQA has identified two areas that the exam will focus on: knowledge/understanding and skills. The skills identified by the SQA are analysis and evaluation. There are very clear definitions in SQA documents about the KU and skills so you have to be sure that you know which is which, otherwise you can bid a fond farewell to your Higher.

Knowledge and understanding

The SQA expects that the knowledge and understanding should be:

- in-depth and should have both factual and abstract information
- relevant to the question
- developed (by providing additional detail, exemplification, reasons or evidence)
- used to respond to the demands of the question.

What this means is that you cannot just shove in some orphaned facts. Orphaned facts, as you will know, are wee floating facts that have nothing much to do with anything in the question. They float about without a care in the world, unbothered by the fact that all they do is use up your time, ink and paper. They are strictly banned when you are answering questions in the RMPS Higher exam.

Let's suppose we have a question like

> **Q** How important is the debate about the existence of God?

and the following opens up the answer:

In-depth:

The existence of God has been a key debate for many centuries for religious people and philosophers alike. The ancient Greeks wondered about whether such a being could exist and came to a variety of conclusions. Some of these conclusions were picked up by Christian philosophers like Thomas Aquinas who formulated his famous Quinquae Vaie based on the ideas of the ancient Greeks.

Wee orphan:

The existence of God has always been a puzzle for humanity. Thomas Aquinas developed ideas from Greek philosophy to prove his belief in God. Thomas went to the University of Naples and at the age of 19 decided that he wanted to become a Dominican priest although he spent much of his time teaching at various universities throughout Europe.

This is a nice bit of depth because it gives a background which says that debates about the existence of God were not exclusive to Christians and then it links the key Christian writer with the Greeks and uses the technical term for Aquinas' arguments. If you take this information out of the answer, the answer will become poorer. The information is needed because it makes a factual point clear.

Starts well, the point is clearly relevant to the question.

And here we have the wee orphan. It is terrific that Thomas went to university and probably had a great time at all the freshers' weeks but the information is not relevant to the question. You could exclude this information and it would make no difference to the answer. This is a sign that it is a wee orphan.

You can see here that, although the answers are the same length, the relevance and depth of them is different. Important questions to ask yourself when you are developing factual information are:

- Is the information relevant to the question?
- If the information is removed from my answer, will it make any difference?
- What am I going to do that makes the information relevant to the question?

To be safe you should really be using your knowledge and understanding skills to tee up an analytical or evaluative point. By doing this you will avoid having wee orphaned facts and you will maintain a focus on the question. Here is how it can be done using the example above:

The existence of God has been a key debate for many centuries for religious people and philosophers alike. The ancient Greeks wondered about whether such a being could exist and came to a variety of conclusions. Some of these conclusions were picked up by Christian philosophers like Thomas Aquinas who formulated his famous Quinque Viae based on the ideas of the ancient Greeks.

This is all factual information, which then needs to be used to make a point.

This is clear evidence that the existence of God has never been something that has been pushed into the background of human thought.

> *Just as it was a significant issue to the ancient Greeks and then, later, to Christian Europe with an obligation being placed on people to accept his existence, so it was an important issue in the Enlightenment as new thinkers swept away old ideas and atheism could, at last, challenge the control that religion had over its followers.*

Using more factual information and some pretty good analysis the candidate goes on to expand on the point. Note the use of 'important issue' – this is a reference back to the question to remind the marker that the answer is on track. You can see a clear relationship between the first and second paragraph whereas with the wee orphan example above it is hard to see where the candidate will go after giving the information about Aquinas' background.

How many marks are available for KU?

The exam claims that around 60% of the marks available are for KU. This is kind of good news because it means that you can get some credit for using factual information. However, the hard bit is what you do with the KU; it has to be relevant and you have to use it to show how much you understand the issue. Simply listing facts or writing about facts that are unrelated to the question will get you no marks at all. Furthermore, the exam does not allow any scope at all for questions like:

- what is or what are?
- describe ...
- give a description ...

Things you need to know, avoid and look out for when using KU in questions

To provide in-depth KU in questions you should know:

- examples from real life
- different religious views on the matter
- different non-religious views on the matter
- some key background information
- some sources.

To provide in-depth KU in questions you should avoid:

- giving personal opinions
- saying that all religious/non-religious people believe the same
- irrelevant background information
- going off at tangents.

To provide in-depth KU in questions you should be on the look-out for:

- chances to quote from scripture or individuals – they get you marks
- the skill identified in the question (i.e. is it analysis or evaluation?)

- opportunities to check the relevance of your KU with the question
- how many times you have used wording from the question (if you have never used it, chances are that your answer and your KU in particular might not be relevant).

General advice on skills questions

The SQA has identified analysis and evaluation as the skills they are going to examine in Higher RMPS. The wording used in the arrangements can be quite hard to get your head round so, unlike the KU, there is not going to be a cutting and pasting job done here to explain them. Let's look at analysis first.

Analysis
It involves where possible and appropriate:

- showing links between different bits of information or viewpoints
- explaining similarities and differences between different bits of information and viewpoints
- explaining consistencies and inconsistencies in different bits of information and viewpoints
- explaining consequences or implications of different bits of information and viewpoints
- understanding what is behind an individual's or organisation's response to a belief, practice or issue.

It's a bit of a list but basically all it is wanting you to do is show that you know what is happening, what could happen and why it is happening. Let's imagine a question like

 Analyse the arguments surrounding the death penalty.

First thing to note is that the question could be as stark and bare as this so be prepared for this approach. As with the KU you need to be careful you have no wee orphaned facts because, more often than not, they will lead you off in the wrong direction. You can have wee floating analytical points just sitting there staring at you in much the same way as you stare at your RMPS teacher when they try to get a discussion going first thing in the morning.

Good answer:

Many religious people are against the death penalty because they believe that life is sacred. This belief in the sanctity of life often comes from scripture or example. In the Old Testament we are told in the 10 commandments that it is wrong to kill so this forms the basis of anti-death penalty views among Jews, Christians and Muslims who happen to believe that the death penalty is wrong. The Buddha taught non-violence and non-harm which again meant that Buddhist countries could not adopt the death penalty since it would involve going against the teaching of the Buddha. In Christianity Jesus' teaching on turning the other cheek and loving enemies echoes the need to respect life found elsewhere in religious cultures.

Factual statement so the next thing is to show how it can be supported.

Showing awareness of the background to the belief – nice one.

OT identified as the source of the belief so this uses a source and shows similarities between religions.

Another similarity identified and also a consequence of the belief.

A nice wee conclusion to the point.

Oh dear oh dear answer:

Many religious people are against the death penalty because they believe that life is sacred. In the Old Testament we are told in the 10 commandments that it is wrong to kill. In Christianity Jesus' teachings tell us we need to respect life. Jesus did not kill anyone. So nobody should of killed him.

Not related to anything. Both points are statements of fact and are not analysis.

But he might have been tempted had he been forced to read this stuff.

The word is 'HAVE', not 'of'. 'Of' is not a verb so a plea to everyone: say and write should or could 'have' not 'of'. Grrrr.

Analysis question stems

The SQA has a helpful list of question stems which might be used in the exam. The list is not exhaustive so don't sit there with a confused look on your face if none of the stems on the list appear. The table below shows some possible question stems and includes those used in the SQA list; some blank boxes have been left at the bottom for when you have an empty house and invite your pals round for a RMPS Question Stem Nite (alternative spelling of 'night' used to make it sound even more fun).

Question stem	Meaning
Explain, give an explanation ...	give a reason as to why something is the way it is or why someone has a particular view
Why might/do ...	give reasons for something
Compare and contrast ...	give similarities and differences between two or more positions
What is ... the problem with/the issue with ...	give a reason as to why something is the way it is or why someone has a particular view
How is ... similar to ...	give similarities and differences between two or more positions
Explain the main influences on ...	give the reasons why individuals believe or do certain things
Explain the consequences of believing/doing ...	what happens as a result of a belief, view or practice
Analyse ...	wide open stem which is more or less asking you to explain the backgrounds, connections/ importance of beliefs, practices
Explain the connection between ...	how are beliefs, practices and ideas connected
Analyse the differences/similarities between ...	looking for you to identify them and explain what they are
Explain the importance of ...	looking for you to show that you know why something is or isn't important in a religious, moral or philosophical issue
In what ways ...	wants you to explain something or other; be careful not to give a simple description

Things to you need to know, avoid and look out for when using analysis in questions

To provide in-depth analysis in questions you should know:

- ways in which beliefs, practices or viewpoints are connected
- background information on beliefs, practices and viewpoints
- the reasons behind different beliefs, practices and viewpoints

- similarities and differences in beliefs, views and practices
- some quotes
- strengths and weaknesses in beliefs, views and practices
- to always refer back to the question
- to use words or phrases from the question.

To provide in-depth analysis in questions you should avoid:

- giving personal opinions
- saying that all religious/non-religious people believe the same
- irrelevant background information
- going off at tangents
- too much description.

To provide in-depth analysis in questions you should be on the look-out for:

- chances to quote from scripture or individuals – they get you marks
- the skill identified by the question stem
- opportunities to check the relevance of your analysis with the question
- how many times you have used wording from the question (if you have never used it, chances are that your answer and your analysis in particular might not be relevant).

Evaluation
The SQA tells us that evaluation questions involve 'making a judgement based on criteria'. Let's re-phrase that 'making a judgement or measurement'. All this really means is that you are expected to be able to express your own view or make some kind of judgement on an issue. However, this is not as easy as it sounds and it is probably the kind of question where people can lose a lot of cheap marks.

The SQA goes on to tell us that evaluation answers will have to be reasoned and that your judgements will be required on, for example:

- The relevance and usefulness of beliefs, views and practices
- Positive and negative aspects of beliefs, views and practices
- Strengths and weaknesses of beliefs, views and practices
- Presenting an overall view of a question or issue.

This list is not exhaustive and later on you will see how varied these questions can be.

At Higher level you need to work on your evaluation. It is not good enough just to say, 'I think there is no God because there is no proof'. Yes, it's a statement with a reason but it does not really say much and would not score any marks. One way of avoiding shallow evaluation is to think of three levels of conviction (as in 'conviction' not as in the criminal convictions of shoplifting or wearing black socks and sandals).

Level one: CONVINCE YOURSELF. This is the easiest level of argument. Here you would think of a belief and convince yourself it is true. This does not require much depth because the only person you have to convince is yourself and you really don't have to justify the view much.

'Abortion is okay because the embryo is not human and a woman's rights must be respected.'

Level two: CONVINCE A FRIEND. This is a bit harder. You have to use some stronger evidence and be prepared for a debate. The debate you will have is in-depth but not too critical because your friend will listen to what you have to say and will not be too sore on your evidence or your belief. They will be on your side and have a respect for your beliefs and your reasons for them. They will probably not make you feel defensive and on the whole give you an easy ride.

An example of a level two argument might be something like

'Abortion is okay because the embryo is not human and a woman's rights must be respected. For example in their earliest stages embryos do not feel pleasure or pain and therefore do not possess attributes that you would expect human beings to have. You cannot then put their rights above those of a woman who will have a sense of pain and pleasure because surely those who can experience this have more of a right to life than those who do not.'

Level three: CONVINCE AN ENEMY. This is the hardest level of all. You have to convince someone who is going to show you no mercy. Someone who is going to disagree with you or pick holes in your argument at every opportunity. You are going to have to use forceful, well-supported arguments to convince your nemesis that you are right and they are wrong.

An example of a level three argument might be something like

'Abortion is okay because the embryo is not human and a woman's rights must be respected. For example in their earliest stages embryos do not feel pleasure or pain and therefore do not possess attributes that you would expect human beings to have. Medically, there is no consensus among doctors about when or how much pain a foetus can experience. So if there is no medical evidence then we have to put the rights of a woman above those of a foetus because she will have a sense of pain and pleasure. She is a sentient being. If you fail to do this, you are putting women on the level of non-sentient beings and basically saying that they have no more right to a choice than say, a honey-bee. Therefore abortion is okay because while pro-choicers do not completely deny the rights of the embryo or the foetus, they recognise the clear and inviolable rights of a woman to choose her way of life.'

Aye, very good, and your point is? The point is that in evaluation questions where you are asked to make a judgement or state a view on something you have to go in and CONVINCE AN ENEMY. Taking this approach means that there is a greater chance that you will build your evaluative point up rather than leaving it at shallow level one, CONVINCE YOURSELF. You can see from the worked examples above that CONVINCE AN ENEMY always has you thinking of what the enemy might say to criticise your argument so you have to dig a bit deeper and produce evidence to convince them that what you are arguing is right.

Of course, convincing people in real life does not necessarily work out like this but for our purposes, and for something that is easy to remember when developing an argument, the 3 Cs can be a useful tool in improving your answer. So, when you have your next RMPS Evaluation Party at Amy's empty, invite some people who are your enemies and just watch your amazing powers of persuasion using:

The 3 Cs

Convince Yourself
Convince a Friend
Convince an Enemy

Evaluation question stems

As with analysis there are a number of possible ways an evaluation question can be phrased and some of these are listed in the table below.

Question stem	Meaning
How valid is ...	Questions like this will usually have some kind of statement before them. The statement can look for you to defend, criticise or give an overview of some point of view.
To what extent/How far do you agree ...	Questions like this will usually have some kind of statement before them. The statement can look for you to defend, criticise or give an overview of some point of view. Don't be fooled by the 'you agree' bit, the main thing is to get over the key issues regardless of your own personal view. Whether the question is 'to what extent' with or without the 'you agree' the answer will be the same.
Evaluate ...	Traditionally candidates have messed up this question. This is asking you to make a judgement about the issue. Very often candidates just give more description or background to questions like this – WRONG! You have to make a judgement on the issue in the question.
How relevant/effective ...	Looks for you to pass comment on whether or not a belief, practice or viewpoint is of any use or has any meaning today.

(continued)

Question stem	Meaning
Discuss/Comment ...	Looks for you to write about the issues surrounding a viewpoint, belief or practice. Don't fall into the trap of simply describing. You need to make some kind of a judgement here because this question stem is looking for you to evaluate.

Things you need to know, avoid and look out for when using evaluation in questions
To provide in-depth evaluation in questions you should know:

- background information on beliefs, practices and viewpoints
- the relevance of beliefs, practices or viewpoints
- the strengths and weaknesses of beliefs, practices and viewpoints
- the positive and negative features of beliefs, practices and viewpoints
- some sources
- to state clear and developed reasons for your views
- to ask yourself who your viewpoint would convince – you, a friend or your enemy?
- to always refer back to the question
- to use words or phrases from the question
- at least two points of view on the issue
- to always make some kind of judgement.

To provide in-depth evaluation in questions you should avoid:

- ranting
- saying that all religious/non-religious people believe the same
- irrelevant background information
- going off at tangents
- too much description.

To provide in-depth evaluation in questions you should be on the look-out for:

- chances to quote from scripture or individuals – they get you marks
- the skill identified by the question stem
- opportunities to check the relevance of your evaluation with the question
- how many times you have used wording from the question (if you have never used it, chances are that your answer and your evaluation in particular might not be relevant).

Skills questions will often involve some kind of statement followed by the analysis or evaluation question. Just to make things complicated the analysis and evaluation questions will be divided up in the exam like this:

World Religion: Always 2 × 10-mark questions, one evaluation and one analysis.

Morality and Belief: Always 2 × 10-mark questions, one evaluation and one analysis.

Religious and Philosophical Questions: Always one 20-mark question with AE combined.

It's time for another RMPS party but not at Amy's this time because her dad went mental at the amount of revision notes left about the place with grammar howlers on them. It's Michael's turn this time for an empty because his parents are quite hip and cool and don't mind RMPS Higher parties at all. The rules are simple:

1. Take your *Grade A Booster* to Michael's house in a plain blue carrier bag (the ones commonly used in corner shops) and conceal it between a bag of Tangy Toms and a large bag of Minstrels.
2. Carefully tear this page out of the book and cut the questions below into strips (thus rendering the book unusable for future candidates and making me more money in royalties).
3. Place the strips onto the Twister mat in the open plan lounge/kitchen (you can play Twister after doing this if you have the energy).
4. Put an 'A' beside those stems that you think are analysis and an 'E' against those that are evaluation.
5. Turn Higher Biology candidates away from the door because this is for RMPS people only.
6. After two hours add up the points and share out the Tangy Toms and Minstrels.
   (a) How might religious people respond to this statement?
   (b) To what extent is this true?
   (c) How far do you agree?
   (d) Why might religious people agree with this statement?
   (e) Explain why some religious people would disagree with this statement.
   (f) How might some religious people support this view?
   (g) Why might some religious people criticise this view?
   (h) Explain how this statement might be defended by religious people.
   (i) Explain how one secular view you have studied would respond to this statement.
   (j) To what extent is this true?
   (k) How far do you agree?
   (l) Why might there be agreement with this statement?
   (m) Explain why some religious people would disagree with this statement.
   (n) Why might some people support this view?
   (o) Why might some people criticise this view?

(p) Explain how this statement might be defended by religious people.

(q) Explain a secular response to this statement.

(r) Why might this be considered a weakness of religious arguments against whatever?

(s) Explain the evidence that could be used to support this secular argument as a strength of the whatever.

(t) How justified is this claim?

(u) In relation to whatever, explain the responses religious people might have to this statement.

Answers

			(u) analysis
(q) analysis	(r) analysis	(s) analysis	(t) evaluation
(m) analysis	(n) analysis	(o) analysis	(p) analysis
(i) analysis	(j) evaluation	(k) evaluation	(l) evaluation
(e) analysis	(f) analysis	(g) analysis	(h) analysis
(a) analysis	(b) evaluation	(c) evaluation	(d) analysis

Know your skills

One of the key things the SQA says about performance is the quality of evaluation skills and the difficulty that candidates seem to have in recognising what skills they are using. There is a way round this and it is to know the words and phrases to use when you are using different skills. There are dozens you can use and the table below highlights just a few of them. Get to know what verbs, phrases or words you use for each skill. A good way to do this is to wait until your RMPS teacher-legend is giving you a lecture about attendance/latecoming/homework/snoring when you are sleeping, and to shout out when they are using different skills:

Teacher-legend: **The fact is** that you are late and you haven't done your homework

You: KU!

Teacher-legend: **The reason for this** is that you are lazy and disorganised.

You: Analysis!

Teacher-legend: **This is a serious disadvantage because** you will miss vital work, and as a consequence, fail the exam.

You: Evaluation!

Teacher-legend: I will have to contact your parents and report this.

You: Empty threat!

Teacher-legend: Are you going to stop that, it's getting a bit wearing?

You: Closed question. Grade Booster says not to do that ...

You get the idea!

Knowledge and Understanding: being able to show that they know and understand beliefs, ideas, concepts and issues through descriptions of facts and relevant information.	Analysis: being able to show that they can pull apart a belief, make connections between beliefs, explain consequences, explain issues, explain implications.	Evaluation: being able to make a judgement or measurement of: strengths, weaknesses, benefits, drawbacks, advantages, disadvantages, impact, importance, effects, veracity, agreement, disagreement.

Refer to the words of the question, e.g. a moral issue arising from ... is ...	However, doing x could result in ... because ...	Rather than doing x ... religious people should ... because ...
One way Buddhists practise meditation is ... Another is ...	One way practice/ viewpoint X links with practice/ viewpoint Y is ...	A strength of this belief/ practice/viewpoint/ argument is ...
One key principle is ...	Some people think that ...	One weakness of this belief/practice/viewpoint/ argument is ...
An example of this is ...	Nevertheless there are consequences ... because ...	Another strength/ weakness etc.
One religious viewpoint on X is ...	It could allow x because ... it says in y ... which means ...	However under certain circumstances x is acceptable because ...
A secular view is ...	A consequence of this might be ... another could be	This is the most popular stance because ...
The Buddha said / the Bible states (or other source) ...	One way this source can be interpreted is ...	I think a benefit of this is ... because ...
Hindus believe ...	As a result of this ...	I think a disadvantage of this is ... because ...
X think this is an issue because ...	This is an example of x because ...	The most prominent issue is ... because ...
Other Jews believe ...	This is related to ... because ...	I think there are advantages and disadvantages of this ...
55% of people ...	An implication arising from this is ...	I agree to a certain extent, because ...
Christians believe that ...	They think this because ...	An implication of X is ... This is a possible weakness because ...
The Bible describes x as ...	This is because ...	This is very important/ a key issue because ...

(continued)

This is also called …	This results in …	Christians would disagree strongly because …
There is also the fact that …	This means that … explanation	This is important/ significant because …
X tells us that …	An interpretation of this passage could be …	A view of x would be that x is more effective than y because …
X is one example of …	This shows …	Belief X is very significant because …
To explain: …	This means that …	A negative way this might affect Buddhists is …
This can/does/often include …	This shapes Muslim views …	X is very important to Y because …

A few things to remember

Before we finish with the basic stuff there is some other basic stuff that you really ought to know. Some of it might be screamingly obvious to you but to some others it is not. Even the most sensible of pupils can do some crazy things in the Higher RMPS exams.

A few must dos

- You must check what sections you are doing and perhaps have them tattooed onto some part of your body that you can see.
- You must make an attempt to answer all of the questions in the sections you have to do. If you miss a question out then you are certain to get zero, zilch, nada, nowt. If you make an attempt at the question then you never know, you have nothing to lose.
- If you do not know what a question is about, go on and do other questions, don't just sit there biting your lip. If at the end of this you still do not know what it is about and no words ring a bell at all, write about something that has not turned up in other questions – again, you never know and markers have to read everything you write.
- Make sure you know a few quotes or individuals or organisations that have said something about the issues you have covered – these can pick up extra marks if they are well used.
- Cover all topics in all the units you have done when you are revising.
- If you make a point, you must support it with either evidence or argument.
- Refer back to the question to keep yourself relevant.
- Remember to learn the stems that tell you to analyse or evaluate or both.

A few 'don't be a daftie' tips

- Do not answer all the questions in the exam paper, because you have not studied all sections.
- Do not get confused between the Existence of God and Origins. There is much overlap in content but the question angles can be different.
- Do not go daft on descriptive information. A good rule to have is one fact for every two analytical or evaluative points.
- Do not miss out questions – always make an attempt.
- Do not panic. Take your time and do the questions you can do; once you get started you often find that the flow of knowledge soon comes.
- Do not write five or ten lines and expect to get many marks for it. The minimum you should be writing for a 10-mark essay is probably around 350 words which is about the size of one sheet of A4 lined paper or two pages in an SQA answer booklet.

In case of emergency

There are two emergencies that can happen in Higher: (a) you have not a single clue about how to answer a question; (b) time is running out.

What not to do

- Panic. Leave a space, go on and do other questions that you can do.
- Leave. This is running away from the problem – once you leave the exam room it is all over for you.
- Miss a question out. If you write nothing, you will get nothing. If you write something then who knows what could happen?
- Phone a friend, go for 50/50 or ask the invigilators. There are rules against this somewhere.
- Stare. Do not sit and stare at the question, that will only make you feel worse – you need to do something, either break the question down or move on to a new question or stick pins in the doll you have made of your RMPS teacher.
- Write a letter. Do not waste your time writing a wee letter to the marker explaining your predicament. Markers have hundreds of questions to mark and will not have the time to waste on your epistle.

Clueless

- Look back to see what topics you have already answered questions on. Whatever topic is missing, write anything about it that you know.
- If you do not understand a statement, try to write it down in your own words – do not just sit and stare at it. Do it word by word. Once you have done that start writing the answer but start by saying what you think the statement means. There's always the chance that your understanding of the statement is one way of looking at it.

- If you do not understand the meaning of words in a question, find a word or phrase in the question that you do understand and write about it – for example, if 'human origins' is used then just write all you know about Christian and evolutionary beliefs about human origins.
- If none of these work or apply, write about anything – you never know, you might just get lucky.

Timeless

- Check that your desk is in the same time zone as the rest of the class or ask the invigilator if there is going to be any injury time.
- Do bullet points. It just has to be a brief summary of what you planned to write. If it is in your exam book and not scored out by you, the marker will mark it and if your information is correct you will get some marks.

Essay writing

There are loads of websites that tell you how to write good essays. (You'll also find a department in school full of people who will tell you how to write a good essay. This is the English department who can be identified by their floppy hats, wilting rose in one hand and a collection of Burns Greatest Hits in the other.) These different sources will give you many suggestions as to how to write a good essay but the basic ideas are pretty much the same.

Step 1 – Understanding the question

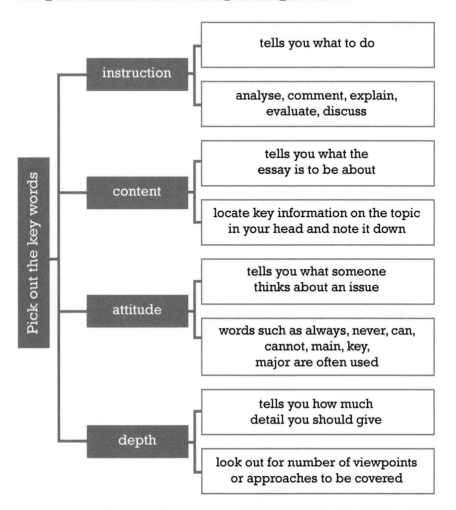

33

Try this:

See if you can pick out the key words in the questions below, and just because I am nice I will do the first one for you:

Why might some religious people disagree with scientific views on the origins of the universe?			
instruction	depth	attitude	content
It's looking for you to explain the reasons behind the belief	It's looking for you to focus on one side of the argument	It's telling you that the side you have to look at is the one that disagrees with science	It's wanting you to write about scientific views of the universe and why some religious people disagree with it

Wasn't that fun? Now try the same thing with the questions below. They are from different units and topics within the course but that should not matter; it is the key words you are looking for and if you can do it for options that are not yours then you can do it for any option:

- Does religion provide a satisfactory explanation for the origins of the universe?
- 'The biblical account of creation should not be compared with scientific accounts of the beginning of the universe. Their purposes are quite different.'
  To what extent do you agree?
- 'Nobody knows where the universe came from. It is all guesswork.' Discuss.
- 'The teleological argument proves beyond all doubt that God exists.'
  Evaluate this statement.
- Why is the existence of suffering and evil used to deny the existence of God by some people?
- If there was no freewill, what difference would it make to human existence?
- Analyse the views of one secular response you have studied to imprisonment.
- Why are there concerns about the death penalty?
- Why should stereotyping be a concern for religious people?
- Analyse the concerns some religious people have about same-sex relationships.
- Compare the views of one secular response to gender equality with that of one religion you have studied.

- To what extent is the 'slippery slope' argument against the use of embryos successful?
- Why is non-voluntary euthanasia considered to be more of a moral issue by some people than voluntary euthanasia?
- Explain two weaknesses of moral arguments against opt out systems of organ donation.
- 'Wars in themselves are not wrong but the way they are fought might be.'
  To what extent do you agree?
- Compare religious and secular views on the use of WMDs.
- 'There is nothing attractive in the belief that we have no soul.'
  Explain Buddhist views on this statement.
- How important is the practice of non-attachment in tackling the Three Root Poisons?
- Why is original sin such an important aspect of Christian teaching?
- Explain how Christians overcome the challenges of following Jesus' example in the 21st century.

Step 2 – Planning the essay structure

The standard approach used since the beginning of time is:

- Introduction
- Body
- Conclusion.

It is not an earth shattering, cosmos changing revelation to tell you that you need to keep the structure of the essay really tight, whether it is an analysis or evaluation 10 marker, or an analysis and evaluation 20 marker essay. Lose the shape and you lose the thread, lose the thread and you lose the question, lose the question and you lose the marks, lose the marks and you lose the life-long respect of your RMPS teacher but, at the same time, boost sales of this book because you'll tell everyone it was right and you wish you had taken its advice.

The introduction

This lets the reader know that you understand the question, what you are going to say and what your view is going to be. It gives the reader your plan of attack because it looks forward to what you are going to write about. The reader should have a pretty good idea of what is to come after reading your introduction and of course be displaying symptoms of a frenzy of fascination and excitement similar to the time when your RMPS teacher is opening up his or her Christmas presents from the RMPS Higher class.

The body

This is the meaty bit. This is where you actually answer the question using your ideas, arguments and evidence. You need to remember the 3Cs here and ask, 'is my argument strong enough to convince my enemy that I am right?' Your points need to be well organised and this is where you have a choice. You can either have a PEE or make a MESS.

You can PEE all over your essay and, for once, this will be seen as a good thing. The formula is quite simple: **P**oint...**E**xplain...**E**xample. Let's expand on that a bit: you make your point, and then you explain your point before finally giving an example to support your point.

The other thing you can do is make a MESS of your answer (tears rolling down my cheeks as I write).

Make a statement about the question or the quote that is used in it.

Explain what your statement means.

Support your statement with evidence and/or arguments.

Summarise your point with reference to the question.

Neither of these is original. The PEE can be found on many websites but the MESS is the property of my colleague. Those of you who are in you early thirties and are sitting Higher RMPS for the 14th time will remember in the first edition of the book my colleague was Miss C. Russell who demanded a menshie in the book should I use her idea. I obliged. In the reprinted edition I updated her marital status to Mrs C. Howie and promised to provide another update in my next book. Well, here it is ... the MESS was created and devised by Mrs C. Howie, mother of Hamish Russell Howie (who in 2029 will be cringing as he reads this book in Higher RMPS). Mrs. Howie plans to have another eleven children so further updates will be provided in future reprints. (Reprint update: all is well in the Howie household.)

The conclusion

Conclusions can be a bit of a pain. They usually involve a summary of what you have already said and then a few final thoughts which get the marker swooning over your insight. In truth, markers often find that very few additional marks are added on for the final conclusion because it has all been said before. If you are able to apply some new kind of supported insight as part of your conclusion then that might pick up something, but go for a measured comment, not some outrageous statement that you cannot support.

Step 3 – Writing the introduction

This is the part of the essay that so many people agonise over. They try to be controversial. They try to use a dictionary definition of a word or phrase. They try to think up some quote they learned off by heart when preparing for the exam. Sometimes these strategies work, sometimes they don't. The introduction is really your opportunity to show the marker two key things:

1. You understand the question.
2. You know how you are going to tackle the question.

Keep it simple. Don't get too elaborate or creative in the introduction, keep that for later on in the essay. Let's have an example or two of introductions:

Q Explain the importance of the Sangha to Buddhists today.

A decent introduction:

The Sangha is a key feature of Buddhism today both for the laity and for monks. Its importance is probably greater in Therevada Buddhism because of its belief that arhats alone can achieve Nibbana. In this essay I will explain the importance of the Sangha in Mahayana Buddhism in terms of the role it plays in the life of laity. I will also explain its role in Therevada Buddhism and explain why its role might well be of greater importance in this branch of Buddhism. My essay will show that the Sangha has a key role to play in the major traditions of Buddhism today, having a major impact on both the laity and the monks.

Shows you know what the Sangha is and that you understand the question.

The basic structure of the essay is stated, now all you have to do is keep to it!

Stating what your conclusion will be is a good way of keeping both yourself and the marker on track.

A dire introduction:

I will talk about the Sangha and its importance in this essay. The Sangha is the Buddhist community. The Sangha is all Buddhists but most often people associate it only with monks. It is very important to Buddhists and wider society because it is a place where you can go and chillax. The Buddha lived in a monastery so that shows its importance and only monks can attain Nibbana which is why it is important.

No you won't! Pens don't talk and neither should you in an exam.

Aye, but where are you going with this?

Chillax? Hate that word. Ten marks off.

No idea where this essay is going and I have to look back at the question to remind myself of what it is about. This is a nightmare.

Q 'Murderers should be executed.'
To what extent do you agree?

A decent introduction:

Those who kill should be killed by the state. This is a hugely controversial statement because there is such a wide range of responses to it; all very passionate. On the one hand there are those who see that the sanctity of life is of paramount importance and life cannot therefore be taken in any circumstances. On the other hand there are those who say that by taking a person's life individuals forfeit their own right to life. It is clear that these two sides are so far apart that they will never agree. In my essay I aim to show that there is a compromise position where both the sanctity of life is protected and the need for justice is achieved. This will be done by analysing and evaluating the respective arguments and then, drawing on their strengths, a compromise will be proposed.

Shows right away that you get the issue by changing the words round a little.

Shows that you have a good grasp of the issue.

Great summary of the two overall positions.

Now you're telling the examiner that you have found a way round the problem of these two opposite positions.

Bog standard and safe way to finish off the intro.

A dire introduction:

I believe very strongly that murderers should be executed. I mean, everyone knows what is right and what is wrong and murderers must surely know that killing someone is wrong. There are some mental cases that maybe should not be executed but it might put them out of their misery if they are and they can't help killing people. The death penalty is a very controversial issue because a lot of people disagree about it but I feel strongly that killers should be killed.

It's ok to give your opinion but this person has turned their introduction into the body of the essay.

No statement of intent here. It is all over the place. This is a classic error – launching headlong into the issue rather than pulling back a bit and thinking how you are going to answer the question.

Step 4 – The body of the essay

This is the part of the essay where the action happens. This is where you pick up the marks, not the introduction and not the conclusion. Here. In a 10-mark essay you are not expected to write ten separate points and in a 20-mark essay you are not expected to write twenty points. In the 10-mark essay you are looking at making 3–4 main points and in the 20-mark essay, probably about 6–8 main points.

You need to think about how you are going to score big points here and this is where making a MESS or having a PEE comes in (or out as the case may be).

Q Explain the ways in which Jesus affects the lives of Christians today?

A decent body point:

I stated earlier that Jesus' death and resurrection have a large impact on Christians today because many of them try to follow the example that Jesus set. | Good to refer to previous points made in the essay. You have made your statement.

This can be seen in the work of World Vision who do much to help street children around the world. Jesus worked with the outcasts of society in his time and fearlessly stood up for them. The adulteress on the verge of execution was one such example. Jesus went against convention of the time and challenged the prejudices against her. In the same way World Vision stands up for those children who are homeless and rootless. | You've gone on to explain your point and in so doing have given examples too.

They say that they 'are committed to following the teaching and example of Jesus Christ in his identification with those who are poor, vulnerable or forgotten.' This is precisely what Jesus did and the thousands of Christians who support or work for World Vision are making Jesus' example one that affects their lives and the lives of others | Now you've used a source to back up your explanation and set up your summary of the point.

because if the effect was only on the lives of individual believers, Jesus would almost certainly have had something to say about that. So, as far as setting an example goes, Jesus' concern for outcasts is one that is copied by World Vision and other Christian groups like the Salvation Army, Christian Aid and Tearfund. There is no doubt that without Jesus' inspiration these groups would not exist and that with his inspiration they are changing lives. | Rounded off nicely with a summary of the point, which also adds a bit more depth to the answer. This paragraph would probably pick up 4 marks or so. Do this three times in a 10 marker or six times in a 20 marker and you'll be laughing!

Q To what extent is science a threat to religious beliefs about the origins of life?

A dire body point:

My first point would be that religions have no proof that God made the universe*. Science has Big Bang and evolution and it is more believable than the Bible stories or other mythologies which could not have happened*. The Big Bang is what made the universe and evolution is what made life.* Scientists have done experiments and have proved it whereas religious people have no proof that God did any of it*. As Dawkins said, 'Biology is the study of complicated things that have the appearance of having been designed with a purpose.'*

Wrong! There is proof, it's just that you don't accept it!

Statement made, nothing to support it in the following lines.

Repetition.

Good quote and it is a good idea to use quotes like this to reinforce or sum up a point. Problem here is that it is hanging out there in the middle of nowhere, not clearly linked to anything else that has been written.

The paragraph is too short and this is always a sign that candidates have not thought things through. With a paragraph this length the candidate is going to need another ten of them to have any chance of getting more than about 12/20. Really weak effort.

Step 5 – Conclusions

The exam expects candidates to draw personal and reasoned conclusions. This can be done in two ways. Most people will draw conclusions throughout their essay (if they follow the excellent instructions in this book) and some will pack all their conclusions into the final paragraph. Either way is fine but what most people find is that they draw conclusions as they go along and then sum them up in the last paragraph or two thereby repeating what they spent the essay telling the marker. If something new is said it will get credit but in practice very few people add anything new and the main purpose of the final concluding paragraph is just to round things off tidily – which is fine.

So, how do you draw a conclusion? Here's how:

Q To what extent can religious people support retributive forms of punishment?

A brilliant conclusion to a point:

Therefore, Christians can make strong cases for and against retributive punishments. The arguments stated earlier suggest that there is biblical support for both responses so much*

Clear conclusion, now we need to see some reasoning

depends on what parts of the Bible individual Christians want to believe. For those in favour of retributive punishments, as pointed out earlier, there is much to support this view in the Old Testament while those who prefer a more forgiving approach would look to the example of Jesus in the New Testament. Neither side is wrong in their response to retributive punishment but both sides believe that their case is stronger than the other.

— One bit of reasoning

— Another bit of reasoning

— Reinforcement of the conclusion

It is necessary therefore to consider non-biblical teaching to see if it provides a clearer picture of the extent to which Christians can support retributive forms of punishment.

— Introduction to the next point

A mince conclusion to a point:

Therefore, Christians can make strong cases for and against retributive punishments. Some are for it and some are against it. It is up to them what they think but in any case religion does not matter these days because nobody listens to out of touch religious people.

— Clear conclusion

Yes, we know that. Heard you the first time.

Off on a rant here. Say this in class if you like but don't put it into the exam.

So there you go, now you know how to break down a question and write an essay. The important thing to remember is that the essay writing skills you use in RMPS are exactly the same as the essay writing skills you use in English. You would never write a three paragraph essay in English; same for RMPS. You need to remember that you have to 'work' the points you make and not just leave a point hanging there with no real depth to it. If you end up doing that, you will be finished the exam in record time and probably get a record low score as well!

Judging your essay

It is really difficult to know how well you have done in an essay. You will know from your folio in English it is sometimes difficult to understand exactly how the marks are awarded. It is the same in RMPS.

The marking instructions for the SQA specimen paper, exemplar paper and past papers include useful grids for each type of question to help you gauge the quality of your essay.

A brief explanation

We are now going to have a look at every section of the paper and how you can prepare your analysis and evaluation for each of the topics you have studied. Most topics are in this book but some are on the Leckie & Leckie website as free downloads because there is not enough paper in the world to do every topic in this book and, apart from anything else, the weight of the book would dislocate your shoulders if all topics were included. The topics not in this book are: Hinduism; Islam; Judaism; Sikhism; Religion, environment and global issues; and Miracles. You can download a chapter for each of these topics from the Free Resources page of the Leckie & Leckie website here: www.leckieandleckie.co.uk/page/Resources.

Course content

The SQA's approach to giving content to courses is to give very broad headings. The reason this is done is to give teachers as much freedom as possible to teach what they want under each heading. This has a couple of implications for the exam and for this book:

- Exam questions will probably be pretty broad in order that questions can capture the general areas studied in each topic. They will probably not be too specific, except when they refer to topics that are actually listed in the content document. If you are bored, you can go to the SQA website and download a document called 'Course Assessment Specification' and in this document you get a list of the various aspects that each topic covers.
- You might find that there are exemplar questions given in the following chapters and panic because you have not covered the stuff in your course. Don't panic. The exemplars can be adapted to suit the course content you have covered so don't go into your next RMPS class accompanied by lawyer, a writ for negligence and an ASBO for the teacher (the ASBO could maybe stay, but not the writ).
- I have followed the same pattern for each topic. First is the content of the unit which has simply been cut and pasted from the SQA document. Second is the general question area. Third is what you need to know, avoid and look out for. Fourth is the different approaches questions can take either through statements and a question or direct questions that just get straight to the point. I've actually made the statements and questions a bit harder than you might get in the exam because Leckie & Leckie have called this book 'Grade A Booster' (aye, nae pressure!).
- There is no way that every question angle can be covered, especially when, in 2015, the exam is brand new. In time, when this book is in its 5th reprint (after successfully being made into a boxset to rival *Breaking Bad*) more question angles will become apparent,

but in the first two or three years there is going to be some guesswork. Hopefully, the people writing the questions will use this book to create their questions, thus making it an even bigger seller and having '#1 International Best Seller' on the front of it. This is the dream.

- After receiving this book at school, or successfully bidding £5,000 for a signed copy at an antiquarian book auction in Larkhall, you should check with your teacher to ensure that there are no changes to course requirements. It is possible that, as experiences of the exam grows, SQA might modify course requirements from time to time.

- **World Religion.** In the World Religion unit the headings, as already said, are very broad. Under each heading there will be some key concepts that your teacher will go over with you. These concepts are ones that could well have specific questions on them in the exam so be prepared to answer 10-mark questions on specific concepts under the general heading. The reason the concepts are not in the exemplar questions is that there may be some concepts that your teacher chooses not to cover and I don't want you going into class and pushing my fine book in their face while screaming, 'You've missed stuff out! You're gonna cost me my Higher. All my hopes of starting off the world's next new religion after studying sociology for four years at Aberclyde have been ruined by your incompetence!' Having experienced this many times myself it is not a place I would want your 'legendary' RMPS teacher to go. If your teacher is 'cool' and glories in that description then they deserve all they get.

- **Use of sources.** You will find that in your internal assessment there are five assessment standards all related to an analysis of sources that 'inform' beliefs and practices. You will have had great fun working on the source and been surprised at how quickly time went by as you were working on it. Let's be clear – it is a good thing to be able to use sources accurately and effectively. However, it is a bad thing to overload on sources.

Buddhism

SQA Course Assessment Specification

Section 1: World Religion

In each world religion, the beliefs, practices and sources are closely related and interconnected. All learners should be able to:

- present in-depth factual and abstract knowledge and understanding of religious sources, beliefs and practices.
- analyse the implications of living according to religious sources, beliefs and practices in the contemporary world.
- evaluate the significance and impact of religious sources, beliefs and practices in the contemporary world.

Learners are not required to learn specific sources for each religious belief and practice. However, learners should be able to use examples of sources that inform beliefs and practices, where appropriate.

Learners may answer questions in the context of a denomination or tradition within the religion selected for study. This should include knowledge and understanding of differences in practices and related beliefs within the religion or tradition studied.

Part A: Buddhism
Beliefs:

- Nature of existence
- Nature of human beings
- Life of the Buddha
- Nibbana
- Kamma
- Dhamma.

Practices:

- The Eightfold Path
- Meditation
- Sangha
- Ten Precepts.

Sources:

- Examples of relevant sources of authority which inform the beliefs and practices.

Analysis approaches

Issue: Explanation of beliefs/practices

Angles

- Background to beliefs/practices
- Development of beliefs/practices
- Role of the belief/practice today.

You need to know (describe):

- detailed information about each belief or practice
- sources which would highlight certain aspects of the beliefs/practices.

You need to be able to explain (analyse):

- how the belief/practice developed
- the role the belief/practice plays in the religion today
- any other beliefs/practices that help make sense of the one you are explaining
- sources which would highlight certain aspects of the beliefs/practices.

You need to avoid:

- simple general descriptions of the belief/practice – this is Higher, you know
- including information about the belief/practice which is not needed to answer the question
- brief answers – 10 marks we're looking for here so that means a fair amount of writing.

You need to look out for:

- alternative spellings of beliefs/practices; SQA will always use the spelling noted above but books or notes you have may use different spellings
- questions that focus on one belief/practice only – you need to be able to write a 10-mark essay on it hence the need to have detailed information
- the question stem – make sure that the question is analysis.

Question approaches
Many of these questions can be adapted simply by inserting different beliefs and practices into the question.
- 'The life of the Buddha is an example to all Buddhists.'
  Explain why the Buddha's life is viewed in this way.
- In what ways do Buddhists understand the nature of existence?
- Choose one Buddhist belief you have studied and explain its role in Buddhism.

- Explain Buddhist beliefs about Nibbana.
- Explain ways in which Buddhist beliefs help Buddhists overcome suffering.
- What views do Buddhists have about the nature of human beings?
- In what ways do Buddhists put the Ten Precepts into practice?
- 'Buddhism calms individual minds.'
  Explain the ways in which Buddhist practices develop calmness in individuals.
- Analyse the key features of Buddhist practices.
- Choose one Buddhist practice you have studied and explain its role in Buddhism.

Issue: Importance of beliefs/practices

Angles

- Background to beliefs/practices
- Development of beliefs/practices
- Role of the belief/practice today.

You need to know (describe):

- detailed information about each belief or practice
- sources which would highlight certain aspects of the beliefs/practices.

You need to be able to explain (analyse):

- their importance to followers and in wider society
- the role the belief/practice plays in the religion today
- any other beliefs/practices that are affected by the one in question
- sources which would highlight certain aspects of the beliefs/practices.

You need to avoid:

- simple general descriptions of the belief/practice – this is Higher, you know
- including information about the belief/practice which is not needed to answer the question
- simply describing the belief/practice – you need to write about its importance
- brief answers – 10 marks we're looking for here so that means a fair amount of writing.

You need to look out for:

- alternative spellings to beliefs/practices; SQA will always use the spelling noted above but books or notes you have may use different spellings
- questions that focus on one belief/practice only – you need to be able to write a 10-mark essay on it hence the need to have detailed information
- the question stem – make sure that the question is analysis
- different words that could relate to importance, e.g. significance, role, centrality.

Question approaches

Many of these questions can be adapted simply by inserting different beliefs and practices into the question.

- 'The Buddha is at the heart of everything Buddhists do.'
  Explain why the Buddha is important in Buddhism.
- In what ways is an understanding of the nature of existence important to Buddhists?
- Choose one Buddhist belief you have studied and explain its importance in Buddhism.
- Explain the significance of Nibbana to Buddhists.
- Explain ways in which Buddhist practices are important in helping Buddhists' spiritual development.
- What views do Buddhists have about the importance of the Sangha?
- In what ways do the Ten Precepts influence the way Buddhists live their lives?
- Explain the value of meditation to Buddhists.
- In what ways are Buddhist practices relevant today?
- Analyse the importance of one Buddhist belief you have studied.

Issue: Connections between beliefs

Angles

- Relationship between beliefs
- Conflict between beliefs
- Support between beliefs
- Connections between one belief and others.

You need to know (describe):

- detailed information about each belief
- their importance to followers and in wider society
- the range of connections between beliefs
- sources which would highlight certain aspects of the beliefs/practices.

You need to be able to explain (analyse):

- how beliefs are connected
- whether the connection is necessary
- how beliefs complement or contradict each other
- how connections enhance or impair understanding.

You need to avoid:

- spending most of the essay writing about the separate beliefs; focus on the connections as soon as you can
- including information about the belief which is not needed to answer the question

- simply describing the belief – you need to write about ways in which they are connected
- brief answers – 10 marks we're looking for here so that means a fair amount of writing.

You need to look out for:

- alternative spellings of beliefs/practices; SQA will always use the spelling noted above but books or notes you have may use different spellings
- questions that focus on more than two beliefs
- the question stem – make sure that the question is analysis.

Question approaches

Many of these questions can be adapted simply by inserting different beliefs and practices into the question.

- 'The Buddha is at the heart of everything Buddhists do.'
  Explain ways in which Buddhist beliefs are related to the Buddha.
- In what ways are beliefs about the nature of humanity connected to kamma?
- Choose one Buddhist belief you have studied and explain its connection to other Buddhist beliefs.
- Explain the relationship between Nibbana and kamma.
- Explain ways in which Nibbana is central to Buddhists' beliefs.
- In what ways are Buddhist beliefs of the nature of existence connected to other Buddhist beliefs?
- 'Buddhist beliefs are all interconnected.'
  What evidence is there to support such a view?
- What are the main themes running through Buddhist beliefs?
- Why are Buddhist beliefs about the nature of existence so important?
- Analyse the relationship between two Buddhist beliefs you have studied.

Issue: Connections between practices

Angles

- Relationship between practices
- Conflict between practices
- Support between practices
- Connections between one practice and others.

You need to know (describe):

- detailed information about each practice
- their importance to followers and in wider society
- the range of connections between practices
- sources which would highlight certain aspects of the practices.

You need to be able to explain (analyse):

- how practices are connected
- whether the connection is necessary
- how practices complement or contradict each other
- how practices enhance or impair understanding.

You need to avoid:

- spending most of the essay writing about the separate practices; focus on the connections as soon as you can
- including information about the practice which is not needed to answer the question
- simply describing the practices – you need to write about ways in which they are connected
- brief answers – 10 marks we're looking for here so that means a fair amount of writing.

You need to look out for:

- alternative spellings of beliefs/practices; SQA will always use the spelling noted above but books or notes you have may use different spellings
- questions that focus on more than two practices
- the question stem – make sure that the question is analysis.

Question approaches

Many of these questions can be adapted simply by inserting different beliefs and practices into the question.

- 'All the steps of the Eightfold Path are closely connected.'
  Explain ways in which the steps are connected.
- In what ways are the Ten Precepts related to the Sangha?
- Choose one Buddhist practice you have studied and explain its connection to other Buddhist practices.
- Explain the relationship between the Sangha and kamma and the Eightfold Path.
- Explain ways in which meditation is central to Buddhist life.
- In what ways is meditation connected to other Buddhist practices?
- 'Buddhist practices have a major impact on the lives of Buddhists.'
  What evidence is there to support such a view?
- What are the main themes running through the Ten Precepts?
- What support might there be for the view that Buddhists should carry out all Buddhist practices?
- Analyse the relationship between two Buddhist practices you have studied.

Issue: Connections between beliefs and practices

Angles

- Relationship between beliefs and practices
- Conflict between beliefs and practices
- Support between beliefs and practices
- Connections between beliefs and practices.

You need to know (describe):

- detailed information about each belief/practice
- their importance to followers and in wider society
- the range of connections between beliefs and practices
- sources which would highlight certain aspects of the beliefs/practices.

You need to be able to explain (analyse):

- how practices/beliefs are connected
- whether the connection reinforces the belief/practice
- how practices/beliefs complement or contradict each other
- how practices/beliefs enhance or impair understanding.

You need to avoid:

- spending most of the essay writing about the separate beliefs and practices; focus on the connections as soon as you can
- including information about the belief and practice which is not needed to answer the question
- simply describing the belief and practice – you need to write about ways in which they are connected
- brief answers – 10 marks we're looking for here so that means a fair amount of writing.

You need to look out for:

- alternative spellings of beliefs/practices; SQA will always use the spelling noted above but books or notes you have may use different spellings
- questions that focus on more than two beliefs and practices
- the question stem – make sure that the question is analysis.

Question approaches
Many of these questions can be adapted simply by inserting different beliefs and practices into the question.

- 'The Sangha is where Buddhism thrives best.'
  Explain ways in which the Sangha helps Buddhists develop a greater understanding of their beliefs.

- In what ways are beliefs about Nibbana connected to meditation?
- Choose one Buddhist belief you have studied and explain its connection to one Buddhist practice.
- Explain the relationship between the Ten Precepts and kamma.
- Explain how Buddhist beliefs and practices develop greater spirituality among Buddhists.
- In what ways are the teachings of the Dhamma put into practice?
- Why are the religious practices of Buddhism so important to beliefs?
- Explain the connection between the Eightfold Path and the Buddha.
- Why is it important for Buddhists to practise what they believe?
- Analyse the relationship between a Buddhist belief and a Buddhist practice you have studied.

Issue: Impact of beliefs/practices on followers/wider society

Angles

- Impact on followers
- Impact on wider society
- Reasons behind the impact
- Reasons behind the lack of impact.

You need to know (describe):

- detailed information about each belief/practice
- their impact on followers and on wider society
- the positive and negative impact on followers and on wider society
- sources which would highlight certain aspects of the beliefs/practices.

You need to be able to explain (analyse):

- the reasons behind the impact of the belief/practice
- the role the belief/practice plays in the world today
- any other beliefs/practices that combine to have an impact on the world today
- sources which would highlight certain aspects of the beliefs/practices.

You need to avoid:

- spending most of the essay writing about the separate beliefs and practices; focus on the impact as soon as you can
- including information about the belief and practice which is not needed to answer the question
- simply describing the belief and practice – you need to write about ways in which they impact on society
- brief answers – 10 marks we're looking for here so that means a fair amount of writing.

You need to look out for:

- alternative spellings of beliefs/practices; SQA will always use the spelling noted above but books or notes you have may use different spellings
- questions that focus on more than two beliefs and practices
- the question stem – make sure that the question is analysis.

Question approaches

Many of these questions can be adapted simply by inserting different beliefs and practices into the question.

- Explain the impact the Sangha has on Buddhist society.
- 'Meditation has transformed the lives of many.'
  Explain the ways in which meditation can change individuals.
- Choose one Buddhist belief you have studied and explain its impact on wider society.
- Explain the impact that the Law of Kamma may have on an individual's behaviour.
- Explain how Buddhist beliefs and practices bring benefits to Buddhists.
- In what ways do Buddhists believe the Dhamma offers a better way to live?
- Why are the religious practices of Buddhism so important to beliefs?
- Analyse the impact of the Eightfold Path on the lives of Buddhists.
- Demonstrate ways in which belief in Nibbana affects individual Buddhists.
- Analyse the reasons behind the popularity of meditation.

Issue: Implications of beliefs/practices for followers/wider society

Angles

- Effects of beliefs/practice on society
- Effects of beliefs/practices on followers
- Benefits/drawbacks of the beliefs/practices.

You need to know (describe):

- detailed information about each belief/practice
- the implications of beliefs/practices for followers and wider society
- the variety of different implications that there can be
- sources which would highlight certain aspects of the beliefs/practices.

You need to be able to explain (analyse):

- the reasons behind the impact of the belief/practice
- the role the belief/practice plays in the world today
- any other beliefs/practices that combine to have an impact on the world today
- sources which would highlight certain aspects of the beliefs/practices
- benefits and drawbacks of beliefs/practices.

You need to avoid:

- spending most of the essay writing about the separate beliefs and practices; focus on the implications as soon as you can
- including information about the belief and practice which is not needed to answer the question
- simply describing the belief and practice – you need to write about their implications
- brief answers – 10 marks we're looking for here so that means a fair amount of writing.

You need to look out for:

- alternative spellings of beliefs/practices; SQA will always use the spelling noted above but books or notes you have may use different spellings
- questions that focus on more than two beliefs and practices
- the question stem – make sure that the question is analysis.

Question approaches

Many of these questions can be adapted simply by inserting different beliefs and practices into the question.

- Explain the implications of the life of the Buddha for Buddhists.
- What are the implications of Buddhist beliefs about the nature of humanity?
- Choose one Buddhist belief you have studied and explain its consequences.
- Explain the consequences of putting the Ten Precepts into practice.
- Explain the effects meditation should have on an individual.
- In what ways do the teachings of the Dhamma affect wider society?
- Why might belief in kamma affect an individual's view on life?
- Explain the consequences of not putting beliefs into practice.
- 'The individual who believes in the Eightfold Path must be prepared to change the way they live.'
  What effects would you expect to see in the lives of individuals who live by the Eightfold Path?
- Analyse the view that belief in the teachings of the Buddha leads to a better society.

Issue: Different views of beliefs/practices

Angles

- Reasons for different views
- Explanation of different views
- Helpfulness of different views.

You need to know (describe):

- detailed information about each belief/practice
- different views or understandings of beliefs/practices from within the religion
- sources which would highlight certain aspects of the beliefs/practices.

You need to be able to explain (analyse):

- the reasons behind different views of the belief/practice
- how different views can aid understanding
- sources which would highlight certain aspects of the beliefs/practices.

You need to avoid:

- spending most of the essay writing about the separate beliefs and practices; focus on the views or understandings as soon as you can
- including information about the belief and practice which is not needed to answer the question
- simply describing the belief and practice – you need to write the views or understandings
- brief answers – 10 marks we're looking for here so that means a fair amount of writing.

You need to look out for:

- alternative spellings of beliefs/practices; SQA will always use the spelling noted above but books or notes you have may use different spellings
- questions that focus on more than two beliefs and practices
- the question stem – make sure that the question is analysis.

Question approaches

Many of these questions can be adapted simply by inserting different beliefs and practices into the question.

- Explain the reasons behind the view that the Buddha is a great role model for Buddhists.
- What views do Buddhists have about attaining Nibbana?
- Choose one Buddhist belief you have studied and explain different understandings of it.
- Why might some Buddhists feel that the Ten Precepts are too hard to practise?
- 'Kamma is a negative influence on society.'
  What reasons might there be for holding such a view?
- 'The religious practices of Buddhism belong to the museum.'
  What points would be raised in a debate about this statement?
- What reasons would be given in support of the relevance of Buddhism today?
- Explain why there might be different understandings of beliefs in Buddhism.

Evaluation approaches

Of all the kinds of question you will meet, those which lend themselves best to having a statement followed by a question are the evaluation questions. So, because of that, a wee change in tack here. There will be a number of statements listed below. In most cases the beliefs or practices will be interchangeable. If you are studying for your prelims during the Christmas holidays you will find that RMPS charades is great fun. Simply mime the beliefs or practices you want in the statement and you'll find the hours will whizz by.

Following the statements there will be the standard 'to what extent' or 'how far do you agree' type questions which can be attached to any of the statements. This revising thing is a lot more fun than people say it is ... sure it is!

Issue: Relevance or importance of beliefs/practices

Angles

- Relevance of a specific belief or practice
- Relevance of beliefs/practices in general
- Importance of specific belief or practice
- Importance of beliefs/practices in general
- Comment on relevance and importance of beliefs/practices.

You need to know (describe):

- detailed information about each belief/practice
- what makes each belief/practice relevant to followers
- what makes each belief/practice relevant to wider society
- how to make a judgement on the relevance with reasons
- sources which would highlight certain aspects of the beliefs/practices.

You need to be able to comment on (evaluate):

- the relevance of different beliefs/practices
- the importance of different beliefs/practices.

You need to avoid:

- spending most of the essay writing about the separate beliefs and practices; focus on the judgement as soon as you can
- including information about the belief and practice which is not needed to answer the question
- simply describing the belief and practice – you need to have some kind of judgement in there
- brief answers – 10 marks we're looking for here so that means a fair amount of writing.

You need to look out for:

- alternative spellings of beliefs/practices; SQA will always use the spelling noted above but books or notes you have may use different spellings
- questions that focus on more than two beliefs and practices
- the question stem – make sure that the question is evaluation.

Question approaches
Many of these questions can be adapted simply by inserting different beliefs and practices into the question.

Statements

- 'Nibbana is not relevant to ordinary Buddhists.'
- 'The Eightfold Path is not practical.'
- 'Meditation brings significant benefits to individuals.'
- 'Wider society has much to learn from Buddhism.'
- 'Buddhist beliefs about the nature of humanity only have relevance for Buddhists.'
- 'If everyone followed the Ten Precepts the world would be a better place.'
- 'Buddhist beliefs are more important than the practices.'
- 'Whether the story of the Buddha is real or mythological is not important.'
- 'The Sangha has been the key to the success of Buddhism.'
- 'Meditation is by far the most important practice in Buddhism.'
- 'Buddhist practices have a significant role to play in wider society.'
- 'Kamma is the key belief in Buddhism.'
- 'There is no more important practice in Buddhism than the Eightfold Path.'

Statement question stems

- How far do you agree?
- To what extent do you agree?
- How fair is this statement?
- To what extent can this statement be justified?
- Discuss.
- Evaluate this statement.

Direct questions

- To what extent do you agree that Nibbana has little relevance to ordinary Buddhists?
- How fair is it to suggest that the Eightfold Path is not relevant anymore?
- Do you agree that the Buddha is as relevant today as he has always been?
- Discuss the view that meditation brings benefits both to followers and wider society.
- To what extent is Nibbana a realistic goal for all Buddhists?
- How important is the Dhamma in Buddhism?
- Evaluate the view that the Ten Precepts are better suited to monks than the laity.
- Discuss the view that the Eightfold Path is as much a moral path as a spiritual path.

Issue: Usefulness of beliefs/practices

Angles

- Practical benefits of beliefs/practices
- Practical issues of beliefs/practices
- Positive/negative views of beliefs/practices
- Comparison of beliefs/practices.

You need to know (describe):

- detailed information about each belief/practice
- what makes each belief/practice useful to followers
- what makes each belief/practice useful to wider society
- how to make a judgement on the usefulness with reasons
- sources which would highlight certain aspects of the beliefs/practices.

You need to be able to comment on (evaluate):

- the reasons behind the usefulness of the belief/practice
- the usefulness of the belief/practice in the world today
- any other beliefs/practices that combine to have an impact on the world today
- sources which would highlight certain aspects of the beliefs/practices.

You need to avoid:

- spending most of the essay writing about the separate beliefs and practices; focus on the judgement as soon as you can
- including information about the belief and practice which is not needed to answer the question
- simply describing the belief and practice – you need to have some kind of judgement in there
- brief answers – 10 marks we're looking for here so that means a fair amount of writing.

You need to look out for:

- alternative spellings of beliefs/practices; SQA will always use the spelling noted above but books or notes you have may use different spellings
- questions that focus on more than two beliefs and practices
- the question stem – make sure that the question is evaluation.

Question approaches
Many of these questions can be adapted simply by inserting different beliefs and practices into the question.

Statements

- 'The Eightfold Path can hardly be described as the middle way since many of the steps are very demanding.'
- 'The practice of meditation brings few benefits to wider society.'
- 'Belief in kamma brings more damage than it does good.'
- 'The moral behaviour taught in meditation is more useful than the meditation itself.'
- 'Buddhist beliefs about the nature of existence provide a greater understanding of our place in the world.'
- 'The monastic Sangha's most useful role is its moral influence on Buddhists.'

Statement question stems

- How far do you agree?
- To what extent do you agree?
- How fair is this statement?
- To what extent can this statement be justified?
- Discuss.
- Evaluate this statement.

Direct questions

- To what extent does the Sangha bring practical benefits to Buddhists?
- Are Buddhist practices selfish or practical?
- How far do you agree that the Dhamma offers practical advice for wider society?
- To what extent does kamma put Buddhists in charge of their own destiny?
- How far do you agree that Buddhist teachings on the nature of humanity offer hope?

Issue: Strengths or weaknesses of beliefs/practices; Positive/negative aspects of beliefs

Angles

- Strengths/weaknesses of specific beliefs/practices
- Positive/negative views of specific beliefs/practices
- Benefits/drawbacks of specific beliefs/practices
- Open general questions on beliefs/practices for the above.

You need to know (describe):

- detailed information about each belief/practice
- the main strengths/weaknesses of each practice/belief for followers
- the main strengths/weaknesses of each practice/belief for wider society
- the positive and negative aspects of beliefs/practices for followers
- the positive and negative aspects of beliefs/practices for wider society

- how to make a judgement on the positive and negative aspects of the religion with reasons
- how to make a judgement on the strengths/weaknesses with reasons
- sources which would highlight certain aspects of the beliefs/practices.

You need to be able to comment on (evaluate):

- the reasons for the strength/weakness/positive/negative
- the fairness of criticisms
- the extent to which the belief/practice is weak/strong/contradictory/positive/negative
- sources which would highlight certain aspects of the beliefs/practices.

You need to avoid:

- spending most of the essay writing about the separate beliefs and practices; focus on the judgement as soon as you can
- including information about the belief and practice which is not needed to answer the question
- simply describing the belief and practice – you need to have some kind of judgement in there
- brief answers – 10 marks we're looking for here so that means a fair amount of writing.

You need to look out for:

- alternative spellings of beliefs/practices; SQA will always use the spelling noted above but books or notes you have may use different spellings
- questions that focus on more than two beliefs and practices
- the question stem – make sure that the question is evaluation.

Question approaches
Many of these questions can be adapted simply by inserting different beliefs and practices into the question.

Statements

- 'Buddhist teachings on the nature of humanity are very negative.'
- 'Buddhist teachings create a sense of hope in individuals.'
- 'The Dhamma has a positive message for humanity.'
- 'The Ten Precepts are limiting and life-negating.'
- 'The Buddha has a negative view of existence.'
- 'The Sangha has shown itself to be a positive influence on wider society.'

Statement question stems

- How far do you agree?
- To what extent do you agree?
- How fair is this statement?

- To what extent can this statement be justified?
- Discuss.
- Evaluate this statement.

Direct questions

- Do you agree that Buddhist teachings on the nature of existence are negative?
- Is it reasonable to argue that Buddhism is a more positive religion than it is a negative one?
- Discuss the Buddhist practices that you consider to bring benefits to followers and wider society.
- Evaluate the impact of Dhamma on Buddhists.

Exemplar analysis points

> **Q** Explain the importance of living morally in Buddhist life.

The Good

Living a moral life is just as important as meditating because all meditation techniques have morals. Mahayana Buddhists have sila which is made up of right speech, right conduct and right livelihood. All of these include moral rules. For example right speech means not saying anything that is bad or untrue. In the Eightfold Path morals are very important too because they are part of the path that leads to enlightenment which is gained through meditation. Some people might say that kamma is important too because it means that you have to be a good person. Living a good life is very important to lay Buddhists in Mahayana because they may not be able to attain enlightenment through meditation.

Good start, 1 mark on the board.

Good point but it needs expansion.

Well explained and it backs up your point.

This doesn't really go anywhere.

Good stuff but needs a bit of expansion to improve the quality. Worth a mark though.

The Bad

A moral life is very important to Buddhism because it is in the Eightfold Path. Meditation is part of the Eightfold Path too so it is just as important because if it was not important then it would not be in the path. Kamma also shows that skilful actions are important for

Good start

Good reasoning but you don't back it up!

being a better person but the Buddha achieved enlightenment by meditating so that shows it is equally important.

> You have good stuff in here but not once did you really expand on any of the points made with the result that this would only be worth 3 or 4 out of 8.

The Ugly

Morals are very important to Buddhists because they have to be moral before they can meditate. Meditation comes in two forms which are vipassana and samatha. Lay people find meditation difficult but arhats can do it because they are full time Buddhists. Lay people have to do good kamma so they will come back as something better in the next life. Morals are more important because they give a person good kamma and if kamma is bad there is no way enlightenment can be attained even if you do meditate. The Five Precepts are morals that Buddhists have and they can be quite hard to follow if you are not a monk. So yes, moral living is much more important than meditation

> Promising start

> Where's this going – maybe we're about to get some acute insights.

> Fair enough but what has this to do with the question?

> Oh no, we're on a tour – the 'Everything I know about Buddhism' tour. Got to hunt for marks now.

> Aha, a mark, hard to find but a perfectly good point.

> Irrelevant.

Exemplar evaluation points

Q Evaluate the impact of Dhamma on Buddhists.

The Good

The impact will vary depending on the culture a Buddhist lives in and on whether or not they are monks or laity. The impact on monks is very clear. It can be seen in their daily routines of prayer, meditations and learning. The whole focus of life in the Sangha is on the Dhamma and on becoming more Buddha-like. The Tricycle Foundation (a group dedicated to promoting Buddhism in the West) say, 'Taking refuge in the sangha means putting your trust in a community of solid members who practice mindfulness together,' which gives a clear view of the extent to which the Sangha is central to the development of faith because of the need to trust in the people in

> Following the MESS steps here. Good stuff. Using a source to support.

the Sangha who will lead the individual to greater depths of insight. Of course, the impact may not be as great in some branches of Buddhism, like Mahayana. The Dhamma impacts on Mahayana Buddhists in a different way. Pure Land has a big focus on individual meditation in the community rather than in the Sangha because when it originated its concern was the ordinary man and not monks. The Dhamma affects Buddhists in places like Korea and Vietnam in a different way because ...

Making a judgement about the consequence. Vital in any evaluation question.

Bringing in another point of view on the same issue to provide contrast and making a MESS too.

Explaining the point and the reasons behind different practice.

And then setting up the next evaluative or judgement point.

The Bad

The impact on monks is very clear. It can be seen in their daily routines. The whole focus of life in the Sangha is on the Dhamma and on becoming more Buddha-like. Some Buddhists say, 'Taking refuge in the sangha means putting your trust in a community of solid members who practice mindfulness together,' which gives a clear view of the extent to which the Sangha is central to the development of faith. Mahayana Buddhists do it differently. Pure Land has a big focus on individual meditation in the community rather than in the Sangha. The Dhamma affects Buddhists in places like Korea and Vietnam in a different way because ...

Aye, but how?

You don't say who said it do you? Just some random Buddhist buying a bag of chips in the Hippy Chippy in Dumbarton. Be clearer!

Following the MESS steps here. Good stuff. Using a source to support.

Aw man, tell us what it means, use the quote.

Why would that be?

And then setting up the next crummy evaluative or judgement point.

The Ugly

The impact on monks is very clear. The whole focus of life in the Sangha is on the Dhamma and on becoming more Buddha-like. Mahayana Buddhists do it differently. Pure Land has a big focus on individual meditation in the community rather than in the Sangha. The Dhamma affects Buddhists in places like Korea and Vietnam in a different way because ...

Is it really? Any chance you can tell us what it is?

We know there is a world ink drought but you won't use up that much by giving us an explanation.

Why would that be?

And then setting up the next crummy evaluative or judgement point which will almost certainly never come.

Christianity

CHAPTER 7

SQA Course Assessment Specification

Section 1: World Religion

In each world religion, the beliefs, practices and sources are closely related and interconnected. All learners should be able to:

- present in-depth factual and abstract knowledge and understanding of religious sources, beliefs and practices.
- analyse the implications of living according to religious sources, beliefs and practices in the contemporary world.
- evaluate the significance and impact of religious sources, beliefs and practices in the contemporary world.

Learners are not required to learn specific sources for each religious belief and practice. However, learners should be able to use examples of sources that inform beliefs and practices, where appropriate.

Learners may answer questions in the context of a denomination or tradition within the religion selected for study. This should include knowledge and understanding of differences in practices and related beliefs within the religion or tradition studied.

Part B: Christianity
Beliefs:

- Nature of God
- Nature of human beings
- Jesus: life, ministry, death, resurrection and ascension
- Kingdom of God
- Judgement.

Practices:

- Individual and community worship
- Living according to the Gospels
- Mission.

Sources:

- Examples of relevant sources of authority which inform the beliefs and practices.

Analysis approaches

Issue: Explanation of beliefs/practices

Angles

- Background to beliefs/practices
- Development of beliefs/practices
- Role of the belief/practice today.

You need to know (describe):

- detailed information about each belief or practice
- sources which would highlight certain aspects of the beliefs/practices.

You need to be able to explain (analyse):

- how the belief/practice developed
- the role the belief/practice plays in the religion today
- any other beliefs/practices that help make sense of the one you are explaining
- sources which would highlight certain aspects of the beliefs/practices.

You need to avoid:

- simple general descriptions of the belief/practice – this is Higher, you know
- including information about the belief/practice which is not needed to answer the question
- brief answers – 10 marks we're looking for here so that means a fair amount of writing.

You need to look out for:

- alternative spellings of beliefs/practices; SQA will always use the spelling noted above but books or notes you have may use different spellings
- questions that focus on one belief/practice only – you need to be able to write a 10-mark essay on it hence the need to have detailed information
- the question stem – make sure that the question is analysis.

Question approaches
Many of these questions can be adapted simply by inserting different beliefs and practices into the question.

- 'The life of Jesus is an example to all Christians.'
  Explain why Jesus' life is viewed in this way.
- In what ways do Christians understand the nature of God?
- Choose one Christian belief you have studied and explain its role in Christianity.
- Explain Christian beliefs about judgement.
- Explain ways in which Christian beliefs help Christians overcome suffering.
- What views do Christians have about the nature of human beings?
- In what ways do Christians put Jesus' teachings into practice?
- 'Christianity brings compassion to individuals.'
  Explain the ways in which Christian practices develop compassion in individuals.
- Analyse the key features of Christian practices.
- Choose one Christian practice you have studied and explain its role in Christianity.

Issue: Importance of beliefs/practices

Angles

- Background to beliefs/practices
- Development of beliefs/practices
- Role of the belief/practice today.

You need to know (describe):

- detailed information about each belief or practice
- sources which would highlight certain aspects of the beliefs/practices.

You need to be able to explain (analyse):

- their importance to followers and in wider society
- the role the belief/practice plays in the religion today
- any other beliefs/practices that are affected by the one in question
- sources which would highlight certain aspects of the beliefs/practices.

You need to avoid:

- simple general descriptions of the belief/practice – this is Higher you know
- including information about the belief/practice which is not needed to answer the question
- simply describing the belief/practice – you need to write about its importance
- brief answers – 10 marks we're looking for here so that means a fair amount of writing.

You need to look out for:

- alternative spellings of beliefs/practices; SQA will always use the spelling noted above but books or notes you have may use different spellings

- questions that focus on one belief/practice only – you need to be able to write a 10-mark essay on it hence the need to have detailed information
- the question stem – make sure that the question is analysis
- different words that could relate to importance, e.g. significance, role, centrality.

Question approaches

Many of these questions can be adapted simply by inserting different beliefs and practices into the question.

- 'Jesus is at the heart of everything Christians do.'
  Explain why Jesus is important in Christianity.
- In what ways is an understanding of the nature of human beings important to Christians?
- Choose one Christian belief you have studied and explain its importance in Christianity.
- Explain the significance of the Kingdom of God to Christians.
- Explain ways in which Christian practices are important in helping Christians' spiritual development.
- What views do Christians have about the importance of Christian mission?
- Explain the value of private worship to Christians.
- In what ways are Christian practices relevant today?
- Analyse the importance of one Christian belief you have studied.

Issue: Connections between beliefs

Angles

- Relationship between beliefs
- Conflict between beliefs
- Support between beliefs
- Connections between one belief and others.

You need to know (describe):

- detailed information about each belief
- their importance to followers and in wider society
- the range of connections between beliefs
- sources which would highlight certain aspects of the beliefs/practices.

You need to be able to explain (analyse):

- how beliefs are connected
- whether the connection is necessary
- how beliefs complement or contradict each other
- how connections enhance or impair understanding.

You need to avoid:

- spending most of the essay writing about the separate beliefs; focus on the connections as soon as you can
- including information about the belief which is not needed to answer the question
- simply describing the belief – you need to write about ways in which they are connected
- brief answers – 10 marks we're looking for here so that means a fair amount of writing.

You need to look out for:

- alternative spellings of beliefs/practices; SQA will always use the spelling noted above but books or notes you have may use different spellings
- questions that focus on more than two beliefs
- the question stem – make sure that the question is analysis.

Question approaches

Many of these questions can be adapted simply by inserting different beliefs and practices into the question.

- 'Jesus is at the heart of everything Christians do.'
  Explain ways in which Christian beliefs are related to Jesus.
- In what ways are beliefs about the nature of humanity connected to the suffering and death of Jesus?
- Choose one Christian belief you have studied and explain its connection to other Christian beliefs.
- Explain the relationship between Kingdom of God and nature of God.
- Explain ways in which judgement is central to Christian beliefs.
- In what ways are Christian beliefs of the nature of human beings connected to other Christian beliefs?
- 'Christian beliefs are all interconnected.'
  What evidence is there to support such a view?
- What are the main themes running through Christian beliefs?
- Why are Christian beliefs about the ascension of Jesus so important?
- Analyse the relationship between two Christian beliefs you have studied.

Issue: Connections between practices

Angles

- Relationship between practices
- Conflict between practices
- Support between practices
- Connections between one practice and others.

You need to know (describe):

- detailed information about each practice
- their importance to followers and in wider society
- the range of connections between practices
- sources which would highlight certain aspects of the practices.

You need to be able to explain (analyse):

- how practices are connected
- whether the connection is necessary
- how practices complement or contradict each other
- how practices enhance or impair understanding.

You need to avoid:

- spending most of the essay writing about the separate practices; focus on the connections as soon as you can
- including information about the practice which is not needed to answer the question
- simply describing the practices – you need to write about ways in which they are connected
- brief answers – 10 marks we're looking for here so that means a fair amount of writing.

You need to look out for:

- alternative spellings of beliefs/practices; SQA will always use the spelling noted above but books or notes you have may use different spellings
- questions that focus on more than two practices
- the question stem – make sure that the question is analysis.

Question approaches

Many of these questions can be adapted simply by inserting different beliefs and practices into the question.

- 'Worship and mission are closely connected.'
  Explain ways in which they are connected.
- In what ways can Christians show a commitment to living their lives as Jesus suggested?
- Choose one Christian practice you have studied and explain its connection to other Christian practices.
- Explain the relationship between the three Christian practices.
- Explain ways in which worship is central to Christian life.
- In what ways is living one's life according to the Gospels connected to other Christian practices?

- 'Christian practices have a major impact on the lives of Christians.' What evidence is there to support such a view?
- What are the main themes running through the expectations of humanity in the Gospels?
- What support might there be for the view that Christians should carry out all Christian practices?
- Analyse the relationship between two Christian practices you have studied.

Issue: Connections between beliefs and practices

Angles

- Relationship between beliefs and practices
- Conflict between beliefs and practices
- Support between beliefs and practices
- Connections between beliefs and practices

You need to know (describe):

- detailed information about each belief/practice
- their importance to followers and in wider society
- the range of connections between beliefs and practices
- sources which would highlight certain aspects of the beliefs/practices.

You need to be able to explain (analyse):

- how practices/beliefs are connected
- whether the connection reinforces the belief/practice
- how practices/beliefs complement or contradict each other
- how practices/beliefs enhance or impair understanding.

You need to avoid:

- spending most of the essay writing about the separate beliefs and practices; focus on the connections as soon as you can
- including information about the belief and practice which is not needed to answer the question
- simply describing the belief and practice – you need to write about ways in which they are connected
- brief answers – 10 marks we're looking for here so that means a fair amount of writing.

You need to look out for:

- alternative spellings of beliefs/practices; SQA will always use the spelling noted above but books or notes you have may use different spellings
- questions that focus on more than two beliefs and practices
- the question stem – make sure that the question is analysis.

Question approaches

Many of these questions can be adapted simply by inserting different beliefs and practices into the question.

- 'The ideals of the Kingdom of God improve life for the community as a whole.' Explain ways in which the Kingdom of God helps promote Christian practice.
- In what ways are beliefs about the Kingdom of God connected to worship?
- Choose one Christian belief you have studied and explain its connection to one Christian practice.
- Explain the relationship between Jesus' life and Christian mission.
- Explain how Christian beliefs and practice develop greater spirituality among Christians.
- In what ways are the teachings of Jesus put into practice?
- Why are the religious practices of Christianity so important to beliefs?
- Why is it important for Christians to practice what they believe?
- Analyse the relationship between a Christian belief and a Christian practice you have studied.

Issue: Impact of beliefs/practices on followers/wider society

Angles

- Impact on followers
- Impact on wider society
- Reasons behind the impact
- Reasons behind the lack of impact.

You need to know (describe):

- detailed information about each belief/practice
- their impact on followers and on wider society
- the positive and negative impact on followers and on wider society
- sources which would highlight certain aspects of the beliefs/practices.

You need to be able to explain (analyse):

- the reasons behind the impact of the belief/practice
- the role the belief/practice plays in the world today
- any other beliefs/practices that combine to have an impact on the world today
- sources which would highlight certain aspects of the beliefs/practices.

You need to avoid:

- spending most of the essay writing about the separate beliefs and practices; focus on the impact as soon as you can

- including information about the belief and practice which is not needed to answer the question
- simply describing the belief and practice – you need to write about ways in which they impact on society
- brief answers – 10 marks we're looking for here so that means a fair amount of writing.

You need to look out for:

- alternative spellings to beliefs/practices; SQA will always use the spelling noted above but books or notes you have may use different spellings
- questions that focus on more than two beliefs and practices
- the question stem – make sure that the question is analysis.

Question approaches

Many of these questions can be adapted simply by inserting different beliefs and practices into the question.

- Explain the impact Christianity has on wider society.
- 'Prayer has transformed the lives of many.'
  Explain the ways in which prayer can change individuals.
- Choose one Christian belief you have studied and explain its impact on wider society.
- Explain how Christian beliefs and practices bring benefits to Christians.
- In what ways do Christians believe the Kingdom of God offers a better way to live?
- Why are the religious practices of Christianity so important to beliefs?
- Analyse the impact of the Gospels on the lives of Christians.
- Demonstrate ways in which belief in the Resurrection of Jesus affects individual Christians.
- Analyse the reasons behind the success of Christian mission.

Issue: Implications of beliefs/practices for followers/wider society

Angles

- Effects of beliefs/practices on society
- Effects of beliefs/practices on followers
- Benefits/drawbacks of the beliefs/practices.

You need to know (describe):

- detailed information about each belief/practice
- the implications of beliefs/practices for followers and wider society
- the variety of different implications that there can be
- sources which would highlight certain aspects of the beliefs/practices.

You need to be able to explain (analyse):

- the reasons behind the impact of the belief/practice
- the role the belief/practice plays in the world today
- any other beliefs/practices that combine to have an impact on the world today
- sources which would highlight certain aspects of the beliefs/practices
- benefits and drawbacks of beliefs/practices.

You need to avoid:

- spending most of the essay writing about the separate beliefs and practices; focus on the implications as soon as you can
- including information about the belief and practice which is not needed to answer the question
- simply describing the belief and practice – you need to write about their implications
- brief answers – 10 marks we're looking for here so that means a fair amount of writing.

You need to look out for:

- alternative spellings of beliefs/practices; SQA will always use the spelling noted above but books or notes you have may use different spellings
- questions that focus on more than two beliefs and practices
- the question stem – make sure that the question is analysis.

Question approaches
Many of these questions can be adapted simply by inserting different beliefs and practices into the question.

- Explain the implications of the life of Jesus for Christians.
- What are the implications of Christian beliefs about the nature of humanity?
- Choose one Christian belief you have studied and explain its consequences.
- Explain the consequences of putting the Kingdom of God into practice.
- Explain the effects worship should have on an individual.
- In what ways do the teachings of the Gospels affect wider society?
- Why might belief in judgement affect an individual's view on life?
- Explain the consequences of not putting beliefs into practice.
- 'The individual who believes in Jesus must be prepared to change the way they live.' What effects would you expect to see in the lives of individuals who live by the Gospels?
- Analyse the view that belief in the teachings of Jesus leads to a better society.

Issue: Different views of beliefs/practices

Angles

- Reasons for different views
- Explanation of different views
- Helpfulness of different views.

You need to know (describe):

- detailed information about each belief/practice
- different views or understandings of beliefs/practices from within the religion
- sources which would highlight certain aspects of the beliefs/practices.

You need to be able to explain (analyse):

- the reasons behind different views of the belief/practice
- how different views can aid understanding
- sources which would highlight certain aspects of the beliefs/practices.

You need to avoid:

- spending most of the essay writing about the separate beliefs and practices; focus on the views or understandings as soon as you can
- including information about the belief and practice which is not needed to answer the question
- simply describing the belief and practice – you need to write the views or understandings
- brief answers– 10 marks we're looking for here so that means a fair amount of writing.

You need to look out for:

- alternative spellings of beliefs/practices; SQA will always use the spelling noted above but books or notes you have may use different spellings
- questions that focus on more than two beliefs and practices
- the question stem – make sure that the question is analysis.

Question approaches
Many of these questions can be adapted simply by inserting different beliefs and practices into the question.

- Explain the reasons behind the view that Jesus is a great role model for Christians.
- What views do Christians have about loving God?
- Choose one Christian belief you have studied and explain different understandings of it.
- Why might some Christians feel that Jesus' example is too hard to follow?
- 'Judgement is a negative influence on society.'
  What reasons might there be for holding such a view?

- 'The religious practices of Christianity belong to the museum.'
  What points would be raised in a debate about this statement?
- What reasons would be given in support of the relevance of Christianity today?
- Explain why there might be different understandings of beliefs in Christianity.

Evaluation approaches

Of all the kinds of question you will meet, those which lend themselves best to having a statement followed by a question are the evaluation questions. So, because of that, a wee change in tack here. There will be a number of statements listed below. In most cases the beliefs or practices will be interchangeable. If you are studying for your prelims during the Christmas holidays you will find that RMPS charades is great fun. Simply mime the beliefs or practices you want in the statement and you'll find the hours will whizz by.

Following the statements there will be the standard 'to what extent' or 'how far do you agree' type questions which can be attached to any of the statements. This revising thing is a lot more fun than people say it is ... sure it is!

Issue: Relevance or importance of beliefs/practices

Angles

- Relevance of a specific belief or practice
- Relevance of beliefs/practices in general
- Importance of specific belief or practice
- Importance of beliefs/practices in general
- Comment on relevance and importance of beliefs/practices.

You need to know (describe):

- detailed information about each belief/practice
- what makes each belief/practice relevant to followers
- what makes each belief/practice relevant to wider society
- how to make a judgement on the relevance with reasons
- sources which would highlight certain aspects of the beliefs/practices.

You need to be able to comment on (evaluate):

- the relevance of different beliefs/practices
- the importance of different beliefs/practices.

You need to avoid:

- spending most of the essay writing about the separate beliefs and practices; focus on the judgement as soon as you can
- including information about the belief and practice which is not needed to answer the question
- simply describing the belief and practice – you need to have some kind of judgement in there
- brief answers – 10 marks we're looking for here so that means a fair amount of writing.

You need to look out for:

- alternative spellings of beliefs/practices; SQA will always use the spelling noted above but books or notes you have may use different spellings
- questions that focus on more than two beliefs and practices
- the question stem – make sure that the question is evaluation.

Question approaches

Many of these questions can be adapted simply by inserting different beliefs and practices into the question.

Statements

- 'Christian mission is not relevant to ordinary Christians.'
- 'The Resurrection is the key belief in Christianity.'
- 'The example of Jesus is not practical today.'
- 'Worship brings significant benefits to individuals.'
- 'Wider society has much to learn from Christianity.'
- 'Christian beliefs about the nature of humanity only have relevance for Christians.'
- 'If everyone followed the example of Jesus, the world would be a better place.'
- 'Christian beliefs are more important than the practices.'
- 'Whether the story of Jesus is real or mythological is not important.'
- 'The example of Jesus has been the key to the success of Christianity.'
- 'Helping others is by far the most important practice in Christianity.'
- 'Christian practices have a significant role to play in wider society.'
- 'The Resurrection is the key belief in Christianity.'
- 'There is no more important practice in Christianity than worship.'

Statement question stems

- How far do you agree?
- To what extent do you agree?
- How fair is this statement?
- To what extent can this statement be justified?
- Discuss.
- Evaluate this statement.

Direct questions

- To what extent do you agree that judgement has little relevance to ordinary Christians?
- How fair is it to suggest that Christian mission is not relevant anymore?
- Do you agree that Jesus is as relevant today as he has always been?
- Discuss the view that worship brings benefits both to followers and wider society.
- To what extent is the Kingdom of God a realistic goal for all Christians?
- How important are the Gospels in Christianity?
- Evaluate the view that the ministry of Jesus has as much relevance today as it has always had.
- Discuss the view that Christian mission has a positive impact on society as whole.

Issue: Usefulness of beliefs/practices

Angles

- Practical benefits of beliefs/practices
- Practical issues of beliefs/practices
- Positive/negative views of beliefs/practices
- Comparison of beliefs/practices.

You need to know (describe):

- detailed information about each belief/practice
- what makes each belief/practice useful to followers
- what makes each belief/practice useful to wider society
- how to make a judgement on the usefulness with reasons
- sources which would highlight certain aspects of the beliefs/practices.

You need to be able to comment on (evaluate):

- the reasons behind the usefulness of the belief/practice
- the usefulness of the belief/practice in the world today
- any other beliefs/practices that combine to have an impact on the world today
- sources which would highlight certain aspects of the beliefs/practices.

You need to avoid:

- spending most of the essay writing about the separate beliefs and practices; focus on the judgement as soon as you can
- including information about the belief and practice which is not needed to answer the question
- simply describing the belief and practice – you need to have some kind of judgement in there
- brief answers – 10 marks we're looking for here so that means a fair amount of writing.

You need to look out for:

- alternative spellings of beliefs/practices; SQA will always use the spelling noted above but books or notes you have may use different spellings
- questions that focus on more than two beliefs and practices
- the question stem – make sure that the question is evaluation.

Question approaches

Many of these questions can be adapted simply by inserting different beliefs and practices into the question.

Statements

- 'The ideals of the Kingdom of God are unrealistic today.'
- 'The practice of worship brings few benefits to wider society.'
- 'Christian mission does more damage than it does good.'
- 'The moral behaviour taught by Jesus brings more to wider society than the spiritual ideals he taught.'
- 'Christian beliefs about the nature of humanity provide a greater understanding of our place in the world.'
- 'The Christian community is a force for good in wider society.'

Statement question stems

- How far do you agree?
- To what extent do you agree?
- How fair is this statement?
- To what extent can this statement be justified?
- Discuss.
- Evaluate this statement.

Direct questions

- To what extent does the Kingdom of God bring practical benefits to Christians?
- Are Christian practices selfish or practical?
- How far do you agree that the ministry of Jesus offers practical advice for wider society?
- To what extent does Christian understanding of the nature of humanity help Christians in daily life?
- How far do you agree that Christian teachings on the nature of humanity offer hope?

Issue: Strengths or weaknesses of beliefs/practices; Positive/ negative aspects of beliefs

Angles

- Strengths/weaknesses of specific beliefs/practices
- Positive/negative views of specific beliefs/practices

- Benefits/drawbacks of specific beliefs/practices
- Open general questions on beliefs/practices for the above.

You need to know (describe):

- detailed information about each belief/practice
- the main strengths/weaknesses of each practice/belief for followers
- the main strengths/weaknesses of each practice/belief for wider society
- the positive and negative aspects of beliefs/practices for followers
- the positive and negative aspects of beliefs/practices for wider society
- how to make a judgement on the positive and negative aspects of the religion with reasons
- how to make a judgement on the strengths/weaknesses with reasons
- sources which would highlight certain aspects of the beliefs/practices.

You need to be able to comment on (evaluate):

- the reasons for the strength/weakness/positive/negative
- the fairness of criticisms
- the extent to which the belief/practice is weak/strong/contradictory/positive/negative
- sources which would highlight certain aspects of the beliefs/practices.

You need to avoid:

- spending most of the essay writing about the separate beliefs and practices; focus on the judgement as soon as you can
- including information about the belief and practice which is not needed to answer the question
- simply describing the belief and practice – you need to have some kind of judgement in there
- brief answers – 10 marks we're looking for here so that means a fair amount of writing.

You need to look out for:

- alternative spellings of beliefs/practices; SQA will always use the spelling noted above but books or notes you have may use different spellings
- questions that focus on more than two beliefs and practices
- the question stem – make sure that the question is evaluation.

Question approaches
Many of these questions can be adapted simply by inserting different beliefs and practices into the question.
Statements

- 'Christian teachings on the nature of God are too hard for ordinary people to understand.'
- 'The greatest strength of Christianity is its founder.'

- 'Christian teachings on the nature of humanity go against human instinct and cannot be trusted.'
- 'Worship's great strength is its contribution to the Christian community.'
- 'The demands of the Kingdom of God have more strengths than weaknesses.'
- 'Christian teachings on the nature of humanity are very negative.'
- 'Christian teachings create a sense of hope in individuals.'
- 'The Gospels have a positive message for humanity.'
- 'The Kingdom of God is limiting and life-negating.'
- 'Jesus has a negative view of existence.'
- 'Christian mission has shown itself to be a positive influence on wider society.'

Statement question stems

- How far do you agree?
- To what extent do you agree?
- How fair is this statement?
- To what extent can this statement be justified?
- Discuss.
- Evaluate this statement.

Direct questions

- Are positive views of the Resurrection justified?
- How fair is it to suggest that Christian teachings on the nature of humanity are negative?
- What do you consider to be the key strengths and weaknesses of Christianity?
- Discuss the view that the main weakness of Christianity is its negative view of humanity.
- Do you agree that Christian teachings on the nature of humanity are negative?
- Is it reasonable to argue that Christianity is a more positive religion than it is a negative one?
- Discuss the Christian practices that you consider to bring benefits to followers and wider society.
- Evaluate the impact of Christian mission on Christians.

Exemplar analysis points

> **Q** Explain the importance of Jesus' suffering and death for Christians.

The Good

The suffering and death of Jesus is hugely important for Christians aiming for salvation. The first point is that without the suffering and death of Jesus there can be no salvation.

Danger! Could end up with evaluation here because she is saying 'hugely important'.

Various scholars like Calvin and Knox have made a strong case for this saying that belief in Jesus' death and resurrection is vital if a person wants to achieve salvation. It is called 'justification by faith' which means that you must have faith in Jesus' suffering and death as being for our salvation.

Gosh, that was intense. It became analysis very quickly and there were references to a couple of writers. She has followed the MESS methodology well. Good point.

The second point is what Jesus' suffering and death actually achieved. The apostle Paul tells us that Jesus' death and suffering was God sending down his own son in order that our relationship with him could be put right. God and humans were alienated (Adam, Eve and original sin explains how and why) and God needed a new covenant to help us get back on terms with him. This is what Jesus' death and suffering achieved. He died for our sins and if we believe in this then we can bridge the gap with God.

Same drill here. Made a MESS and gave an explanation of how it all worked. No opinions given which is good and the facts are related to the analysis.

The Bad

Jesus' suffering and death is very important. To get to heaven you have to believe in Jesus and what he did so it is important in that way. It is also important because if there was no death and suffering of Jesus then there would be no salvation and we would all go to Hell. Another thing is that we need to believe in the suffering and death of Jesus to get to Heaven.

This is pretty basic but passable. It is a bit of a list and the explanations are thin. You can see how, compared to the good one, this person has said the right things but has not expanded on anything. This is a classic error at Higher.

Some Christians say that it is important to believe in other things and do other things too. The suffering of Jesus is important but it is also important that Christians help other people because that is what Jesus did and that will be important when God judges your life before you get into Heaven. Overall though the importance is very true because it plays such an important part in things like Christian worship, Easter is a time when Christians think a lot about Jesus' suffering.

And then we go flying off on a tangent and turn it into an evaluation question which is not the skill that was being tested.

The Ugly

Salvation is important to Christians because it means that they can get into Heaven and meet up with relatives and friends again. It is important because Christians have to believe in it as part of their faith. Their belief in it would be pointless if there was no salvation.

Eh? This is what you call an irrelevant point. It would get zilch, nada, nuffin.

Exemplar evaluation points

Q 'Christian mission has shown itself to be a positive influence on wider society.' How far do you agree?

The Good

Christian mission has had both a positive and negative impact on the world as a whole. In the 19th century Christian mission was a powerful force for education and health throughout Africa through the work of the likes of David Livingstone. The work of Christian mission saved lives and spread the ideals of education, democracy and equality in areas which were previously difficult to control. On the downside though, Christian mission was used to expand the influence of Europe and the territories of the European super powers of the time. In places like India, mission disregarded the many local religions on many occasions with the result that the native population almost felt like strangers in their own land. It would be unfair to say that mission was a negative thing in the former British Empire because it brought about much good including things like literacy and better trade but the way it was used to cast aside local beliefs, customs and traditions is something that would not be tolerated today.

Both sides mentioned so this is what we should expect to see.

Clear point. Facts are used to make a point about the positive effects of mission.

Negative side given so the aim of this point has been achieved.

A conclusion about the point. Note that no sources are used. This is fine. It is clear that there is a depth of knowledge here that shows the person knows sources without quoting them.

The Bad

The work of Christian mission saved lives and spread the ideals of education, democracy and equality in areas which were previously difficult to control. | Clear point, but it has not been developed.

On the downside though, Christian mission was used to expand the influence of Europe and the territories of the European super powers of the time. | Clear point, but again not developed.

It would be unfair to say that mission was a negative thing in the former British Empire because it brought about much good but the way it was used to cast aside local beliefs, customs and traditions is something that would not be tolerated today. | Conclusion is good but there is not a lot of evidence about how he came to the conclusion. The point is right but the reasons for the judgement have not been developed at all.

The Ugly

The work of Christian mission saved lives and spread good ideals. In places like India, mission disregarded the many local religions. It would be unfair to say that mission was a negative thing in the former British Empire but the way it was used to cast aside local beliefs, customs and traditions is something that would not be tolerated today. | Jumps about too much and does not develop any points in any depth.

Morality and Belief

In the Morality and Belief section there are some wee additional complications thrown in just to annoy you but in particular to annoy your teachers. You have to study religious and non-religious responses to the issue you are studying. Easy peasy, so far, so good. However, you have also to apply what is called a 'key moral perspective' to the issues you have studied. This means that you have to apply utilitarianism or a religious moral perspective to the topic you have studied. It's the same for every unit.

Questions might look something like this:

Q In what ways might utilitarianism be applied to moral issues arising from capital punishment?

The chapters on Morality and Belief have been laid out thus:

- SQA Course Specification
- Issue
- Angles
- You need to know
- You need to be able to explain
- You need to be able to comment on
- You need to avoid
- You need to look out for
- Statements
- Question stems for statements
- Direct questions

It is worthwhile looking at questions in the different chapters because I've tried to vary the approach to questions from time to time. You'll find that most times you can adapt the question to suit your topic.

Religion and Justice

SQA Course Assessment Specification

Section 2: Morality and Belief

All learners should be able to:

- present in-depth factual and theoretical knowledge and understanding of the moral issues within each part.
- present detailed factual and theoretical knowledge and understanding of religious and non-religious viewpoints on different aspects of the moral issues in the part studied. These viewpoints will include: utilitarianism, religious authority.
- analyse the different aspects of the moral issues in the part studied.
- evaluate the religious and non-religious responses to different aspects of the moral issues in the part studied. Learners may answer questions in the context of a denomination or tradition within the religious responses.

Part A: Religion and Justice

- Causes of crime
- Perspectives on punishment: retribution, proportionality, forgiveness
- Approaches to capital punishment
- Sentencing in the UK
- Comparative effectiveness of capital punishment and UK sentencing.

Analysis approaches

Issue: Causes of crime

Angles

- Connection between causes of crime and criminal behaviour
- Influence of the causes of crime on punishment/sentencing
- Reasons for religious and non-religious views of the causes of crime
- Moral issues raised by the causes of crime
- Religious and non-religious responses to the causes of crime
- Responsibility for the causes of crime.

You need to know (describe):

- the causes of crime
- different religious and non-religious views and actions on the causes of crime
- the moral issues raised by the causes of crime.

You need to be able to explain (analyse):

- the reasons behind different responses to crime
- the link between causes of crime and criminal behaviour
- similarities and differences between different approaches to the causes of crime
- how the causes of crime are related to other aspects of Religion and Justice
- the consequences of different causes of crime.

You need to avoid:

- giving the impression that hanging is too good for them
- expressing points of view in analysis questions – even more tempting than missing RMPS Higher last two on a Friday, so be warned.

You need to look out for:

- questions that look like analysis but are not
- the question stems that give you a clue about whether it is analysis or evaluation.

Question approaches

- Explain the connection between criminal behaviour and the causes of crime.
- Give an explanation of the moral implications of the causes of crime.
- Analyse religious responses to the causes of crime.
- Explain the similarities and differences between religious and non-religious responses to crime.
- What are the moral issues that are raised by the causes of crime?
- What reasons are sometimes given for criminal behaviour?
- Explain why the causes of crime raise moral issues.
- What is the importance of understanding the causes of crime?
- Why are the causes of crime considered important in the moral debate surrounding justice?
- Explain different views on the individual criminal's responsibility for crimes.

Issue: Perspectives on punishment: revenge, proportionality, forgiveness

Angles

- Connection between causes of crime and approaches to punishment
- Implications of different approaches to crime
- Reasons for religious and non-religious views on punishment
- Moral issues raised by the different purposes of punishment
- Consistency between religious teaching and different forms of punishment
- Agreement/disagreement between religious and non-religious views of punishment
- Relationship between purposes of punishment and other issues related to justice.

You need to know (describe):

- the different perspectives on punishment
- different religious and non-religious views on punishment
- the moral issues raised by punishment.

You need to be able to explain (analyse):

- the reasons behind different responses to the purposes of punishment
- the link between purposes of punishment and crime levels
- similarities and differences between different approaches to different purposes of punishment
- how the purposes of punishment are related to other aspects of Religion and Justice
- the consequences of different purposes of punishment
- the moral issues raised by different purposes of punishment.

You need to avoid:

- giving the impression that you would personally like to try out some revenge-based punishments on your siblings
- expressing points of view in analysis questions – very easy to do because punishment is a highly controversial issues. Keep disciplined.
- mixing up the different perspectives – common error.

You need to look out for:

- questions that look like analysis but are not
- the question stems that give you a clue about whether it is analysis or evaluation.

Question approaches

- Explain ways in which different purposes of punishment have reduced crime rates.
- Give an explanation of the moral implications of one purpose of punishment you have studied.

- Analyse religious responses to revenge as a purpose of punishment.
- Explain the similarities and differences between religious and non-religious proportionality as a purpose of punishment.
- What are the moral issues that are raised by different purposes of punishment?
- What reasons are sometimes given for forgiving criminal behaviour?
- Explain why the purposes of punishment raise moral issues.
- What is the importance of understanding the purposes of punishment?
- Why are the purposes of punishment considered important in the moral debate surrounding justice?
- Explain the reasons behind the desire for revenge as a purpose of punishment.

Issue: Approaches to capital punishment

Angles

- Connection between causes of crime, approaches to punishment and capital punishment
- Implications of different approaches to capital punishment
- Reasons for religious and non-religious views on capital punishment
- Moral issues raised by capital punishment
- Consistency between religious teaching and capital punishment
- Agreement/disagreement between religious and non-religious views of capital punishment
- Relationship between capital punishment and other issues related to justice.

You need to know (describe):

- the different perspectives on capital punishment
- different religious and non-religious views on capital punishment
- the moral issues raised by capital punishment
- the practice of capital punishment across the world
- justice systems that permit capital punishment
- the methods of capital punishment.

You need to be able to explain (analyse):

- the reasons behind different responses to capital punishment
- the link between capital punishment and crime levels
- similarities and differences between different approaches to capital punishment
- how the purposes of punishment are related to capital punishment
- the consequences of capital punishment
- the moral issues raised by capital punishment
- the possible conflict between justice and capital punishment.

You need to avoid:

- giving gory descriptions of executions; won't get you many marks even if it's fun to write about them
- expressing points of view in analysis questions – very easy to do because capital punishment is a highly controversial issue
- ranting about the death penalty – maybe in some places but not in analysis questions
- taking *Dead Man Walking* into the exam (if you do then use headphones and don't cry out loud).

You need to look out for:

- questions that look like analysis but are not
- the question stems that give you a clue about whether it is analysis or evaluation
- going off at a tangent since capital punishment does dominate this unit even although it shouldn't. What is it with young people and gorefests?

Question approaches

- Explain ways in which capital punishment can be seen as a deterrent.
- Give an explanation of the moral implications of capital punishment.
- Analyse religious responses to capital punishment.
- Explain the similarities and differences between religious and non-religious views on capital punishment.
- What are the moral issues that are raised by capital punishment?
- What reasons are behind religious views that support capital punishment?
- Explain why there is a moral debate about capital punishment.
- Give an analysis of the implications of capital punishment.
- Why are the purposes of punishment considered important in the moral debate surrounding capital punishment?
- Explain the reasons behind the desire for revenge as a purpose of punishment.

Issue: Sentencing in the UK

Angles

- Basis of the UK justice system
- Relationship between UK sentences and purposes of punishment
- Relationship between UK sentences and the causes of crime
- Reasons for religious and non-religious views of UK sentencing
- Moral issues raised by UK sentencing
- Purpose of UK sentencing policies.

You need to know (describe):

- the range of sentences available in the UK
- the application of different sentences in the UK
- religious and non-religious responses to/views of the range and application of sentences in the UK.

You need to be able to explain (analyse):

- the reasons behind different responses to UK sentencing policy
- the link between purposes of punishment and UK sentencing
- similarities and differences between different approaches to UK sentencing
- how UK sentencing might be related to other aspects of Religion and Justice.

You need to avoid:

- going off on a personal rant about wishy-washy liberal approaches to justice (sometimes lining offenders up against a wall for execution is not the answer)
- expressing points of view in analysis questions – easy trap to fall into. If you do evaluation in an analysis question there will no marks for you which means that you will fail the exam which means that you will turn to a life of crime and be used as a case study one day.

You need to look out for:

- questions that look like analysis but are not
- questions that ask for moral views on sentencing; think about the moral issues not the social issues they raise.

Question approaches

- Explain the connection between UK sentencing and the purposes of punishment.
- Give an explanation of the moral implications of UK sentencing.
- Analyse religious responses to UK sentencing policy.
- Explain the similarities and differences between religious and non-religious responses to sentences passed on criminals in the UK.
- What are the moral issues that are raised by multiple life sentences?
- What reasons are sometimes given for sentencing individuals to community service?
- Explain why imprisonment raises moral issues.
- What is the importance of understanding the causes of a crime before sentence is passed?
- Why are UK sentencing policies criticised by some people?
- Explain different views on society's responsibility towards the victim and the perpetrator of the crime.

Issue: Comparative effectiveness of sentencing in the UK and capital punishment

This is an odd aspect of this part because there is not an awful lot to say about it. Furthermore, squeezing moral issues out of it will be no mean feat. For these reasons there are far fewer specific questions on it than in other sections. You will probably find that much of the content here is spread across every aspect of the Religion and Justice issue.

Angles

- UK sentencing policy and crime prevention
- The relationship between UK sentences and purposes of punishment
- The relationship between UK sentences and the causes of crime
- The reasons for religious and non-religious views of UK sentencing
- The moral issues raised by UK sentencing and capital punishment.

You need to know (describe):

- the range of sentences available in the UK
- the application of different sentences in the UK
- religious and non-religious responses to/views of the range and application of sentences in the UK
- before and after statistics for UK crime rates (since the abolition of capital punishment).

You need to be able to explain (analyse):

- the effectiveness of alternatives to capital punishment
- the link between increased crime rates and crime statistics
- moral issues raised by the abolition of capital punishment
- the humanity of life sentences compared to death sentences.

You need to avoid:

- going off on a personal rant just because you're angry that the RMPS exam is almost always one of the last in the diet
- expressing points of view in analysis questions – easy trap to fall into when you have just watched the last episode of Channel 5's light-hearted *Top 100 Botched Executions* of a Saturday evening.

You need to look out for:

- questions that look like analysis but are not
- questions that ask for moral views on sentencing and capital punishment; think about the moral issues and not the social issues they raise.

Question approaches

- Compare the approaches to justice of countries that do have the death penalty with those that do not.
- What are the moral issues that are raised by the debate about the effectiveness of UK sentencing?
- What reasons are sometimes given for restoring capital punishment in the UK?
- Explain why retributive punishment raises moral issues.
- Why are UK sentencing policies criticised by some people?
- Explain different views on society's responsibility towards preserving the life of the criminal.

Evaluation approaches

Just like in World Religions, evaluation questions lend themselves best to having a statement followed by a question. Like in World Religions we have a change of approach here. There will be a number of statements listed below. In most cases issues and responses will be interchangeable. Just adapt them as you wish. Following the statements there will be the standard 'to what extent' or 'how far do you agree' type questions which can be attached to any of the statements.

Issue: Causes of crime as an explanation for crime

Angles

- Responsibility for crime
- Moral issues raised by the causes of crime
- Moral issues raised by responses to the causes of crime
- Effectiveness of dealing with causes of crime
- Causes of crime as a concern for religious/secular groups.

You need to know (describe):

- why some people reject/accept links between causes of crime and criminal behaviour
- why the causes of crime can be controversial
- four or five points about the causes of crime and related issues to be safe
- what has been done by religious and secular groups to help those affected by the causes of crime, e.g. religious work with addicts, government initiatives in deprived areas
- the successes and failures that have been experienced by these different groups
- why some people feel that tackling the causes of crime is pointless and why some feel that we have a duty to tackle the causes of crime
- what the religious and secular views are – you will find that they are very similar and it is a good thing to point this out
- why religious and secular groups are concerned about the causes of crime.

You need to be able to comment on (evaluate):

- the moral issues raised by the causes of crime
- the moral issues raised by responses to the causes of crime
- the relevance of religious/non-religious views on the causes of crime
- the importance of the causes of crime in the moral debate surrounding justice.

You need to avoid:

- confusing the causes of crime and purposes of punishment (impossible I know but it has been done before!)
- thinking that it is only opinions that are wanted here; religious concerns can be shown by the responses they have.

You need to look out for:

- questions that ask you for a discussion of one particular cause. Make sure you can write in detail about at least three of the causes
- questions that ask for information on this issue – they are probably the trickiest questions in this unit
- questions that ask for a religious view – your answer will contain loads of secular insights which are shared with religious people but, if you can, find a couple of things that are clearly religious.

Question approaches
Statements

- 'The causes of crime are simply excuses for unacceptable behaviour.'
- 'Every criminal has understandable reasons for committing crimes.'
- 'The causes of crime are a concern for everyone.'
- 'Behind every crime there is an individual who has been let down by society.'
- 'Religious responses to crime are weak and ineffective.'
- 'Responses to the causes of crime simply do not work.'
- 'Everyone has a responsibility to tackle the causes of crime.'
- 'The only effective response to the causes of crime is to get tough on criminals.'
- 'Responses to the causes of crime tend to be all talk and no action.'
- 'We should concentrate on punishing criminals, not understanding why they do it.'
- 'You cannot consider how to punish criminals without understanding why they committed their crime.'
- 'The reasons behind someone committing a crime are more important than how we punish them.'
- 'When an individual commits a crime it is always his or her choice to commit the crime.'
- 'Being poor or coming from a difficult background is no excuse for criminal behaviour.'
- 'To be truly forgiving religious people should show great concern about the causes of crime.'

Statement question stems

- To what extent do you agree?
- How far do you agree?
- Is this statement fair?
- To what extent might non-religious and religious people agree?
- How successfully can religious people support this view?
- To what extent might this view be supported?
- Evaluate this statement.
- Discuss.
- How relevant is this view?
- To what extent is this important in the debate about the causes of crime?

Direct questions

- Why should the causes of crime be a concern for religious people?
- To what extent is society to blame for crime rather than the individual?
- How far do you agree that the causes of crime should be considered before deciding on punishment for criminals?
- How effective are religious responses to the causes of crime?
- To what extent are secular responses to the causes of crime successful?
- Do you agree that responses to the causes of crime have limited success?
- Why should the causes of crime be a concern?
- Why do some people consider criminals to be victims?
- To what extent should society be concerned about the causes of crime?
- How far do you agree that crime is down to individuals simply being greedy for something?
- Has religion got anything to contribute to the debate about the causes of crime?

Issue: The purposes of punishment

Angles

- Views of each purpose of punishment
- Purposes of punishment as a religious/secular concern for society
- Moral issues raised by each purpose of punishment
- Strengths and weaknesses of each purpose of punishment
- Implications of each purpose of punishment.

You need to know (describe):

- the good and bad points of each purpose of punishment you have studied
- the successes and failures of each purpose of punishment
- why some people prefer one purpose or combinations of purposes over others
- examples of these benefits, etc., from real life
- your own hand-crafted examples gleaned from the life full of retributive punishment you are currently experiencing at school.

You need to be able to comment on (evaluate):

- religious and non-religious views of each purpose of punishment
- strengths and weaknesses of each purpose of punishment
- the moral implications of each purpose of punishment.

You need to avoid:

- confusing the different purposes of punishment.

You need to look out for:

- questions that focus on one purpose – you need to have loads to write here
- questions that ask you to explain the success or failure of different purposes of punishment.

Question approaches
Statements

- 'Punishment must be just that; painful.'
- 'The punishment should fit the crime.'
- 'Revenge does not work because people still commit crimes.'
- 'Forgiveness is a soft option for criminals.'
- 'Criminals do not need reformed; they need to suffer for their crimes.'
- 'Society must be prepared to give criminals another chance in life.'
- 'Punishment should only be about reforming an individual.'
- 'Criminals should be forgiven for their crimes.'
- 'Punishment does not solve anything.'
- 'Punishment is not for revenge, but to lessen crime and reform the criminal.' (Elizabeth Fry)

Statement question stems

- To what extent do you agree?
- How far do you agree?
- Is this statement fair?
- To what extent might non-religious and religious people agree?
- How successfully can religious people support this view?
- To what extent might this view be supported?
- Evaluate this statement.
- Discuss.
- How relevant is this view?
- To what extent is this important in the debate about the purposes of punishment?

Direct questions

- Why do some people argue that revenge is essential to punishment?
- Explain the weaknesses of proportionality as a purpose of punishment.
- To what extent does forgiveness as a purpose of punishment benefit society?
- How far do you agree that forgiveness as a purpose of punishment fails?
- Do you agree that the most important purpose of punishment is preventing others from committing the same crime?
- How far do you agree that the only purpose of punishment that is morally acceptable for religious people is forgiveness?
- How far can revenge as a purpose of punishment be considered morally right?
- Discuss which purpose of punishment should give society the greatest cause for concern.

Issue: Sentencing in the UK

Angles

- Viewpoints on UK sentencing
- UK sentencing as a concern for society/religion
- Moral issues arising from different sentences
- Religious and non-religious responses to different sentences.

You need to know (describe):

- the different sentences that are used
- the good and bad points about different sentences
- at least a couple of sentences in some depth in case there is a focus on one sentence only
- what the religious and secular views are – you will find that they are very similar and it is a good thing to point this out
- why religious and secular groups are concerned about the sentences handed down.

You need to be able to comment on (evaluate):

- religious and non-religious views of sentencing in the UK
- strengths and weaknesses of sentencing in the UK
- the moral implications of each sentence in the UK.

You need to avoid:

- discussing capital punishment because it is not a punishment that is handed down in the UK.

You need to look out for:

- questions that focus on one particular sentence
- questions that ask for a religious view – your answer will contain loads of secular insights which are shared with religious people but, if you can, find a couple of things that are clearly religious.
- questions that focus on one particular sentence and whether it could be justified by a religious person
- questions about religious and secular reasons for not using certain sentences.

Question approaches
Statements

- 'Community service is good for both society and the criminal.'
- 'Community service is so weak as a punishment it is hardly worth having.'
- 'Imprisonment is seen by many as a soft option.'
- 'Life imprisonment should mean 'life'.'
- 'Fines are the most effective punishment because criminals suffer and the state gets money.'
- 'There is only one suitable punishment for any crime – imprisonment.'
- 'Religious people can only support punishments which show forgiveness.'
- 'Without forgiveness, criminals will never change.'
- 'Religions demands justice. Retribution as a purpose of punishment gives it.'
- 'The first priority of the justice system is to protect the public from criminals.'

Statement question stems

- To what extent do you agree?
- How far do you agree?
- Is this statement fair?
- To what extent might non-religious and religious people agree?
- How successfully can religious people support this view?
- To what extent might this view be supported?
- Evaluate this statement.
- Discuss.
- How relevant is this view?
- To what extent is this important in the debate about UK sentencing?

Direct questions

- To what extent is imprisoning criminals beneficial to society?
- Why is community service sometimes considered to be an inadequate punishment?
- Why should the purposes of punishment be a concern for religious people?
- Why do some religious people argue that revenge is essential to punishment?
- Why do some people consider community service a weak response to crime?
- To what extent should sentencing be a concern of religion?

- Discuss the views of at least one secular response you have studied to imprisonment.
- Do you agree that the most important purpose of punishment is deterring others from committing the same crime?

Issue: Capital punishment

Angles

- Effectiveness of capital punishment
- Religious and non-religious views of capital punishment
- Moral issues arising from capital punishment.

You need to know (describe):

- why capital punishment is seen as effective/ineffective
- the arguments for and against capital punishment
- at least three weaknesses/strengths of each argument
- what the religious and secular views are – you will find that they are very similar and it is a good thing to point this out
- why religious and secular groups are concerned about capital punishment.

You need to be able to comment on (evaluate):

- religious and non-religious views of capital punishment
- strengths and weaknesses of each view on capital punishment
- the moral implications of capital punishment.

You need to avoid:

- getting hooked on just one or two reasons for its effectiveness. There are many reasons for its effectiveness and ineffectiveness but very often candidates end up just writing loads about one.
- generalising religious views – there are many shades of opinion.

You need to look out for:

- questions that link capital punishment to the purposes of punishment
- questions that focus on one particular aspect of capital punishment
- questions that ask for a religious view – your answer will contain loads of secular insights which are shared with religious people but, if you can, find a couple of things that are clearly religious
- questions that focus on one particular reason for having the death penalty and whether it could be justified by a religious person
- questions about religious and secular reasons for NOT using the death penalty.

Question approaches
Statements

- 'To take a life when a life has been lost is revenge, not justice.' (Desmond Tutu)
- 'Taking your life when you have taken the life of another – now that is true justice!'
- 'There is no evidence that the death penalty reduces crime.'
- 'The death penalty removes the problem; it does not solve it.'
- 'The death penalty only works for those who want revenge.'
- 'If the death penalty was a real deterrent then nobody would commit crimes that could result in it.'
- 'Regardless of the method, the death penalty can never be right.'
- 'The death penalty shows that human life **is** sacred.'
- 'The death penalty is more compassionate than life imprisonment.'
- 'The loss of one innocent life to execution is a price worth paying.'
- 'If killing is wrong, it is wrong in all cases and for all reasons.'
- 'The death penalty violates human rights, in a ruthless, absolute and irreversible manner.'
- 'Killing is wrong. It makes no sense that we kill murderers to show them that killing is wrong.'
- 'Religious people cannot support capital punishment.'
- 'By murdering a person, a murderer is showing that he no longer considers life as sacred. For that reason he should be executed.'
- 'The only way to deter murderers is to have the death penalty.'
- 'Any action that causes harm to another individual is morally wrong.'

Statement question stems

- To what extent do you agree?
- How far do you agree?
- Is this statement fair?
- To what extent might non-religious and religious people agree?
- How successfully can religious people support this view?
- To what extent might this view be supported?
- Evaluate this statement.
- Discuss.
- How relevant is this view?
- To what extent is this important in the debate about capital punishment?

Direct questions

- Why do some people consider the death penalty to be effective?
- To what extent is the death penalty successful as a deterrent?
- How far do you agree with the view that the death penalty is only effective as a form of revenge?
- To what extent does the death penalty benefit society?

- Are the concerns about the death penalty valid?
- Why do some people consider capital punishment to be inhuman?
- Giving reasons for your answer, explain why some people consider executions to be humane.
- To what extent do you agree that the death penalty can never be right?
- Evaluate two arguments which support the death penalty.
- How important are human rights in the debate about capital punishment?
- Evaluate the strengths and weaknesses of at least one religious argument used in the debate about capital punishment.
- Evaluate the strengths of at least one secular argument used in the debate about capital punishment.
- Discuss the objections that some people might have to one religious view of capital punishment that you have studied.
- On what grounds might one secular view of capital punishment that you have studied be criticised?
- Discuss the support that can be provided for one religious position on capital punishment

Exemplar analysis points

Q Explain how one moral perspective you have studied might be applied to issues arising from justice.

The Good

> Utilitarianism is based on the principle of performing acts that bring the greatest happiness to the greatest number of people. One issue in justice is that of the purposes of punishment. One purpose of punishment is deterrence which is the idea that any punishment should be designed to prevent more being harmed by crime. This would be approved by utilitarians because the consequence of this is that fewer people would be affected by crime and as a result society would be a happier place.

Simple statement of what utilitarianism is (you have no idea how hard it is to type utilitarianism quickly without making a mistake).

More KU to set up the AE – this kid is good.

Analysis point made.

An even more popular purpose of punishment for utilitarians would be reformation of the convict. This would create greater happiness in society because fewer crimes would be committed, people would feel safer and criminals themselves would have a happier life because they are not caught up in crime. Everyone in reformative punishment benefits so if everyone benefits then happiness will increase.

Same deal here, more of this and it will be up at an A.

The Bad

One issue in justice is the purposes of punishment. One purpose of punishment is deterrence. This would be approved by utilitarians because the consequence of this is that fewer people would be affected by crime.

Another purpose of punishment is reformation of the convict. This would create greater happiness in society because fewer crimes would be committed.

This person is giving themselves a mountain to climb. They are going to run out of info pretty quickly because none of the points are developed or explained and when this happens many people simply don't have enough information to fill an answer.

The Ugly

Deterrence would be approved by utilitarians because it puts people off committing crimes. It also means that you can execute people. People who kill deserve all that they get – a life for a life. Society is better off without them because once a murderer always a murderer. Hannibal Lecter is a good example of this, once a killer always a killer and if he was dead then the whole world would be a happier place.

Misses the point a bit and it is a bit of a rant. Hannibal Lecter isn't real by the way. I think.

Exemplar evaluation points

Q 'All methods of execution are immoral.'
How might a non-religious person respond to this view?

The Good

The statement means that it does not matter what kind of execution is carried out it is still wrong. A lot depends on what you believe about the death penalty. If you believe that the death penalty is wrong then it does not matter what method is chosen. It is wrong. As one opponent in Texas put it, 'This is premeditated, carefully thought out ceremonial killing.' This statement suggests that it is wrong because it is planned and because there is the ceremony of the trial, the appeals and the build up to the execution itself.

> Good start, showing that you know what the statement means.

> No problem with this, good point.

> Good use of quote and it has also been explained to show how it connects with the question.

There are different opinions about the death penalty being moral. In the US some campaigners argue that the death penalty is a cruel and unusual punishment. If it is cruel and unusual then you could say that it is immoral. The problem is that what I might say is cruel and unusual another person might say is ok. Executions could also be immoral because it does not matter what method is used, a human is taking the life of another human and that is wrong. How can killing a killer for killing be moral? There are examples from every type of execution of it going wrong and the person suffering. There are more examples of the innocent being executed and if that is not immoral then what is? Whatever method of execution is used the criminal has to wait for a long time for his death to come. That means he is being deliberately made to suffer or fight for his life – that is cruel and since it does not happen to a lot of people it is also unusual. So that makes the method of execution immoral.

> Good point and very useful to refer to a situation in real life.

> Clocking up these marks now!

> Good question but you did not take it anywhere. Try to avoid rhetorical questions.

> Know what you're trying to say but it doesn't really come off does it?

> Ok, you had to work it a wee bit here and then twist it round to fit the question but you did it well.

On the other hand some non-religious people think execution is a good idea and that lethal injection is the moral way to do it. Most states in the US use lethal injection because *it does not cause the prisoner any pain. This is a moral method because it is humane. He is just put to sleep. It might not be nice to put someone to sleep but it does not make it an immoral method. Some people might even argue that not to make the criminal suffer is immoral. The criminal caused suffering so to be morally fair you have to make sure that he suffers as much as the victim. You could say that certain methods of execution are immoral because they involve making the prisoner deliberately suffer and that to make people suffer is immoral because we should be trying to protect each other from unnecessary suffering.*

Well done, keeping on track by mentioning a phrase from the question. This whole bit would get a mark or so.

Good point and it might get something; it would definitely have got something if you had gone on and explained it a bit.

Good point too but why did you stop there? You could have rounded the whole thing off nicely with a final conclusion. Overall, worth about 75% of the marks.

Excellent answer. Clearly argued with a good balance of evidence and argument. This would score really well in the exam.

The Bad

The death penalty is wrong because you could end up executing an innocent person. You could get the wrong person and put them through all that suffering for something they did not do, that is why the death penalty is wrong. Deathpenaltyinfo.org say that executions are wrong because the different methods can go wrong and can make the criminal suffer more pain than they were meant to. Some people who agree with the death penalty might feel that lethal injection is the only right way to treat a criminal because it is humane and involves no pain whereas other methods of execution can involve a huge amount of pain for the criminal.

People who are against the death penalty would say that all methods of execution are immoral because to take a person's life for any reason is immoral. Just because a person has murdered someone doesn't mean that we then have the right to kill him. If we do not have the right to kill then no method of execution can be moral.

This is not what the question was about. Read it again! You are off track!

Hello-oh! You're still off track. Go back and read the question before it is too late.

Whew! Getting back on track and with a source as well. Good stuff.

Well on track now and possibly a couple of marks here for you.

Taking the opposite view ... good tactic. Another mark here.

Another mark for this point too. This is borderline overall and you made it borderline because you started off by not answering the question. Once you have written your first point for any question, look back at the question, read what you have written and make sure it is relevant.

Good to see an attempt to use sources; that can always pick up marks. Several good points made but the problem is that they have not been supported with evidence or argument. It's a mistake to leave statements unsupported.

The Ugly

If you take a life you should lose your life. I think the execution is right because why should a person live when they have killed someone else? They have taken someone's life so they have given up the right to have their own life. I think that if people were executed for crimes apart from murder that would be wrong. People like drug addicts need to be helped and not executed. Crimes like robbery should mean that people get put in jail. Life imprisonment can work but only as long as it means life. I think that the death penalty is less cruel than life imprisonment because imagine being in prison for your whole life and never having the chance to get out again. So yes, I think that non-religious people would think that methods of execution are immoral.

Wrong approach! Read the question!

Maybe a wee smidgin of a mark here but you're still off track.

What are you on about? You have not mentioned the question once, you're going on about other punishments. This is about the DEATH PENALTY – it is not a chance for you to have a rant.

This is a rant. It is a personal rant against the justice system in the UK. Problem is, the answer is off the mark as a result. Avoid ranting at all costs.

Religion and Relationships

SQA Course Assessment Specification

Section 2: Morality and Belief

All learners should be able to:

- present in-depth factual and theoretical knowledge and understanding of the moral issues within each part.
- present detailed factual and theoretical knowledge and understanding of religious and non-religious viewpoints on different aspects of the moral issues in the part studied. These viewpoints will include: utilitarianism, religious authority.
- analyse the different aspects of the moral issues in the part studied.
- evaluate the religious and non-religious responses to different aspects of the moral issues in the part studied. Learners may answer questions in the context of a denomination or tradition within the religious responses.

Part B: Religion and Relationships

- Religious, moral and legal aspects of marriage
- Nature of relationships: sexuality, love, intimacy
- Perspectives on the roles of men and women
- Gender inequality and exploitation.

Analysis approaches

Issue: Religious, moral and legal aspects of marriage

Angles

- Connection between the religious, moral and legal aspects of marriage (themes within them)
- Influence of religion on marriage
- Reasons for religious and non-religious views on marriage
- Moral issues raised by different types of marriage
- Reasons behind religious and non-religious views of marriage
- Responsibilities of individuals in a marriage
- Place of marriage in society.

You need to know (describe):

- the different types of marriage
- different religious and non-religious views on different types and purposes of marriage
- the moral issues raised by different types and purposes of marriage
- the role of marriage in society.

You need to be able to explain (analyse):

- the reasons behind different responses to different types of marriage
- the connection between religious and non-religious views of marriage
- similarities and differences between different approaches to marriage (and marriage types)
- how the religious, moral and legal aspects of marriage are related to other aspects of Religion and Relationships
- the consequences of different types of marriage.

You need to avoid:

- proposing to the person sitting next to you in the exam if they promise to give you a copy
- accepting a proposal of marriage from the person sitting next to you in the exam because you have given them a copy
- being overly descriptive in your explanations of each type of marriage
- expressing points of view in analysis questions – even more tempting than missing RMPS Higher last two on a Friday so be warned.

You need to look out for:

- questions that look like analysis but are not
- the question stems that give you a clue about whether it is analysis or evaluation.

Question approaches

- Explain the connection between religion and beliefs about marriage.
- Give an explanation of the moral implications of arranged marriages.
- Analyse religious responses to different types of marriage.
- Explain the similarities and differences between religious and non-religious responses to marriage responsibilities.
- What are the moral issues that are raised by different types of marriage?
- What reasons are sometimes given for people not wishing to marry?
- Explain why marriage raises moral issues.
- What is the importance of understanding the purpose of marriage?
- Why are the purposes of marriage considered important in the moral debate surrounding marriage?
- Explain different views on the individual responsibilities in marriage.

Issue: Nature of relationships

Angles

- Role of love in marriage
- Influence of religion on relationships
- Reasons for religious and non-religious views on sexual relationships
- Moral issues raised by different types of sexual relationships
- Reasons behind religious and non-religious views of sexual relationships
- Responsibilities of individuals in sexual relationships
- Perspectives on the role of sex in society today
- Perspectives in religious and non-religious views of sex in society today.

You need to know (describe):

- the different types of love
- the different types of sexual relationship (e.g. heterosexual, homosexual)
- different religious and non-religious views on different types and purposes of relationships
- the moral issues raised by different types and purposes of relationships
- the role of sexual relationships in society.

You need to be able to explain (analyse):

- the reasons behind different responses to different types of relationship
- the connection between religious and non-religious views of relationships
- similarities and differences between different approaches to relationships
- how sexuality is related to other aspects of Religion and Relationships
- the consequences of individual sexuality.

You need to avoid:

- making a wee hearty sign thing with your hands to the invigilators in the pathetic hope they'll give you extra time
- standing up in the exam and announcing your sexual preferences – nobody will notice and that is maybe the problem …
- being overly descriptive in your explanations of each type of relationship
- expressing points of view in analysis questions.

You need to look out for:

- questions that look like analysis but are not
- the question stems that give you a clue about whether it is analysis or evaluation.

Question approaches

- Explain the connection between religion and beliefs about sex.
- Give an explanation of the moral implications of same-sex marriages.
- Analyse religious responses to different types of sexuality.
- Explain the similarities and differences between religious and non-religious responses to sexuality.
- What are the moral issues that are raised by pre-marital sex?
- What reasons are sometimes given for people considering pre-marital sex to be wrong?
- Explain why the issue of marriage and homosexuality raises moral issues.
- What is the importance of understanding human sexuality?
- Why is understanding the nature of love important in understanding human relationships?
- Explain different views on the role and purpose of sex.

Issue: Perspectives on the roles of men and women; Gender roles and exploitation

Angles

- Role of men and women in relationships
- Role of men and women in society generally
- Reasons for religious and non-religious views of the role of women
- Moral issues raised by different roles of men and women
- Responsibilities of men and women
- Perspectives on the role of men and women in society today
- Perspectives on religious and non-religious views of men and women in society today
- Moral issues raised by exploitation of men and women.

You need to know (describe):

- the different types of roles of men and women
- different religious and non-religious views on the roles of men and women
- the moral issues raised by different roles of men and women in society
- the importance of gender roles in society
- different types of gender exploitation.

You need to be able to explain (analyse):

- the reasons behind different responses to inequality based on gender
- the reasons behind different responses to exploitation based on gender
- the connection between religious and non-religious views of gender roles/exploitation/ equality
- similarities and differences between different approaches to gender roles/exploitation/ equality

- how gender roles are related to other aspects of Religion and Relationships
- the consequences of gender equality/roles/exploitation.

You need to avoid:

- being overly descriptive in your explanations of each exploitation and inequality – easy to get lost in descriptions and not focus on the issue in the question
- expressing points of view in analysis questions.

You need to look out for:

- questions that look like analysis but are not
- the question stems that give you a clue about whether it is analysis or evaluation.

Question approaches

- Explain the connection between religion and beliefs about gender roles.
- Give an explanation of the moral implications of gender inequality.
- Analyse religious responses to different types of gender exploitation.
- Explain the similarities and differences between religious and non-religious responses to gender equality.
- What are the moral issues that are raised by gender roles?
- What reasons are sometimes given for people considering gender equality to be wrong?
- Explain why exploitation based on gender raises moral issues.
- What is the importance of understanding gender roles in the moral debate about relationships?
- Why is understanding gender roles important in understanding human relationships?
- Explain different views on the role of men and women.

Evaluation approaches

Just like in World Religions, evaluation questions lend themselves best to having a statement followed by a question. Like in World Religions we have a change of approach here. There will be a number of statements listed below. In most cases issues and responses will be interchangeable. Just adapt them as you wish. Following the statements there will be the standard 'to what extent' or 'how far do you agree' type questions which can be attached to any of the statements.

Issue: Religious, moral and legal aspects of marriage

Angles

- Moral issues arising from different types of marriage
- The sanctity of marriage

- Moral issues raised by divorce and re-marriage
- Protection for males and females within marriage
- Purpose of marriage
- Religious views on marriage
- Non-religious views on marriage.

You need to know (describe):

- religious and non-religious views of marriage
- the roles of men and women in marriage
- different understandings of the purpose of marriage
- reasons behind the sanctity of marriage
- approaches to divorce, both religious and non-religious.

You need to be able to comment on (evaluate):

- the moral issues raised by marriage and divorce
- the moral issues raised by different types of marriage
- the relevance of religious/non-religious views on marriage and its purposes
- the importance of the sanctity of marriage for religious and non-religious people
- the moral issues raised by the sanctity of marriage.

You need to avoid:

- trying to set up a date for two teachers who you think are unmarried at the senior Christmas dance – it's just wrong, okay?
- being overly descriptive when discussing different types of marriage
- thinking that it is only opinions that are wanted here; religious concerns can be shown by the responses they have.

You need to look out for:

- questions that ask you for a discussion of one particular type of marriage. Make sure you can write in detail about at least two types of marriage.
- questions that ask for a religious view – your answer will contain loads of secular insights which are shared with religious people but, if you can, find a couple of things that are clearly religious.

Question approaches
Statements

- 'Marriage has outlived its usefulness.'
- 'No marriage should be forever.'
- 'The purpose of marriage is to provide security for the next generation.'
- 'Divorce should be made as hard as possible.'
- 'Religious responses to divorce are irrelevant. Times have changed.'

- 'There is nothing morally wrong with same-sex marriages.'
- 'Everyone has a responsibility to avoid divorce if at all possible.'
- 'The sanctity of marriage is no longer relevant.'
- 'Marriages are only proper if they involve religious ceremonies and vows.'
- 'We should concentrate more on keeping couples together than making it easy to divorce.'

Statement question stems

- To what extent do you agree?
- How far do you agree?
- Is this statement fair?
- To what extent might non-religious and religious people agree?
- How successfully can religious people support this view?
- To what extent might this view be supported?
- Evaluate this statement.
- Discuss.
- How relevant is this view?
- To what extent is this important in the debate about marriage?

Direct questions

- Why should the causes of divorce be a concern for religious people?
- To what extent is divorce a sign that marriage has lost its importance?
- How far do you agree that same-sex marriages are right?
- How effective are religious responses to different types of marriage you have studied?
- To what extent are non-religious responses to divorce morally acceptable?
- Do you agree that religious views on the purposes of marriage are irrelevant?
- Why should marriage be a concern for all of society?
- Why do some people consider divorce to be wrong?
- To what extent should society be concerned about the causes of divorce?
- How far do you agree that divorce should be easier to obtain?
- Has religion got anything to contribute to the debate about marriage and divorce?

Issue: Nature of relationships: sexuality, love, intimacy

Angles

- Religious and non-religious views on sexuality
- The role of sex in relationships
- Religious and non-religious views of marriage
- Definitions or forms of love
- Relationship between different forms of love
- Importance of love in relationships.

You need to know (describe):

- religious teachings on love, sex and relationships
- non-religious views on love, sex and relationships
- different understandings of love.

You need to be able to comment on (evaluate):

- the role of sex in relationships
- the role of love in relationships
- religious and non-religious views of sex
- views on the purpose of sex.

You need to avoid:

- can't give much advice here without it reading like a script from a *Carry On* film. Sorry.
- having a lack of balance on religious views.

You need to look out for:

- questions that ask about love and sex.

Statements

- 'Sex is only for marriage.'
- 'Religious views on sex are common sense and fair.'
- 'Sex without love is immoral.'
- 'There is no greater quality than love.'
- 'The foundation of all relationships should be love.'
- 'Love is desirable in marriage but not essential.'
- 'Marriage is the only place where true love can exist between two people.'
- 'Same-sex marriage is based on lust not love.'
- 'There is nothing wrong with having casual sexual relationships.'
- 'It is time religion got over its issues with pre-marital sex. It is harmless.'

Statement question stems

- To what extent do you agree?
- How far do you agree?
- Is this statement fair?
- To what extent might non-religious and religious people agree?
- How successfully can religious people support this view?
- To what extent might this view be supported?
- Evaluate this statement.
- Discuss.
- How relevant is this view?
- To what extent is this important in the debate about sexual relationships?

Direct questions

- Why do some people argue that same-sex relationships cannot be allowed?
- Explain the weaknesses of arguments supporting fidelity in marriage.
- To what extent is love equally as important as sex in relationships?
- How far do you agree that casual sex is wrong?
- Do you agree that the most important purpose of sex is the creation of children?
- How far do you agree that the only purpose of sex that is morally acceptable for religious people is procreation?
- How far can same-sex relationships be morally right?
- Discuss why sexual love raises moral concerns.

Issues: Perspectives on the roles of men and women; Gender inequality and exploitation

Angles

- Religious and non-religious views on the roles of men
- Religious and non-religious views on the roles of women
- The impact of different roles of men and women
- The changes taking place in the roles of men and women
- Moral issues arising from equality
- Moral issues arising from different roles of men and women
- Causes of and responses to inequality
- Impact of inequality
- Causes of and impact of exploitation.

You need to know (describe):

- religious and non-religious teachings on the roles of men and women
- moral issues raised by the roles of men and women
- different responses to moral issues surrounding equality
- traditional views v. progressive views of the roles of men and women
- different forms of exploitation within relationships and society as a whole.

You need to be able to comment on (evaluate):

- the impact of different roles on society
- the role of equality in debates about the roles of men and women
- religious and non-religious views of the roles of men and women
- the value of different roles
- the value of equality.

You need to avoid:

- confusing questions which ask about inequality within marriage and inequality in society as a whole.

You need to look out for:

- questions that ask about inequality – don't hammer the work of different organisations; that would make your answer very descriptive.

Question approaches
Statements

- 'The traditional role of women is good for families and good for society.'
- 'Religion is a force against equality for women.'
- 'Men are exploited in different but equally wrong ways by women.'
- 'Men and women have different roles but equal status.'
- 'Greater equality between men and women is not necessarily a good thing.'
- 'The exploitation of women is the most important issue in the debate about relationships.'
- 'Women are subjected to more exploitation than men.'
- 'Equality is as important in marriage as love.'
- 'The equality of men and women is not an issue for religion.'
- 'The stereotypes of both men and women are morally wrong.'

Statement question stems

- To what extent do you agree?
- How far do you agree?
- Is this statement fair?
- To what extent might non-religious and religious people agree?
- How successfully can religious people support this view?
- To what extent might this view be supported?
- Evaluate this statement.
- Discuss.
- How relevant is this view?
- To what extent is this important in the debate about equality?

Direct questions

- To what extent is equality a key issue in the debate about relationships?
- Why is there such an emphasis on equality for women?
- Why should the role of women be a concern for religious people?
- Why do some religious people argue that men and women should have different roles in marriage?
- Why do some people consider religious responses to the equality of men and women weak?

- To what extent should the traditional roles of men and women be supported?
- Discuss the views of at least one non-religious response you have studied to the exploitation of women.
- Do you agree that the most important issue in marriage is equality between the man and the woman?

Exemplar analysis points

 Q   Explain different understandings of love.

The Good

> There are several different understandings of love identified by various people. C.S. Lewis wrote about them and identified them as firstly storge.

Good start, source mentioned but nothing was done with it so it wouldn't get any credit.

> Storge comes from a Greek word meaning 'affection'. This is a bit like a natural love. It is a type of love that does not involve a commitment but which allows us all to get along with each other and respect each other's space. For example, in school there would be riots if we did not have a basic affection for each other. We do, so this means that we can quietly co-exist, giving people their space, putting up with their faults, not smashing into them in the science corridor for a laugh. It is like an instinct where you are born and somehow know you have to co-operate with people to get on. This kind of love has the least commitment in any way but it does have a basic commitment, almost like a kind of empathy for understanding others.

Definition given and now the explanation has to be worked.

And there it is. Just look at the various angles taken here. There are examples, implications, deeper definitions – all of which clearly show that this candidate has a deep understanding of what this definition of love is about. This is how you 'work' a point.

The Bad

> Storge comes from a Greek word meaning 'affection' . This is a bit like a natural love. It is a type of love that does not involve a commitment but which allows us all to get along with each other and respect each other's space. For example, in school there would be riots if we did not have a basic affection for each other. This kind of love has the least commitment in any way.

See here, see how next to nothing has been expanded. The answer has become really basic. It's not wrong, it's just basic and won't get much if it continues in this vein.

The Ugly

The best form of love is agape. This is the kind of love that makes marriages work. All the other types of love are really shallow. Storge is just affection and is just trying to get on with people. Eros is the sex one and philo is friendship which is probably the one we use most but not on Facebook because on that the friendships we have are probably more like storge than philo although some people use Facebook for eros type love which is against the law.

Whit are ye oan aboot? This is just weird. Avoid this person at all costs.

Exemplar evaluation points

 'Sex without love is a meaningless experience.'
Discuss religious and non-religious views of this statement.

The Good

Religions are not against sexual relationships. *Many religious people enjoy a full sex life with their partner so the first point is that religion is not against people having sex.* *The problem for religion is how it is used.* *In general, religions do not approve of sex outside marriage and consider that marriage is the only legal outlet for our sexual desires.* *More traditional religious views of sex would argue that* *sex outside marriage has a bigger risk of being meaningless because there is not the same commitment that you would get in a marriage.* *For example, in Christian teaching, marriage involves the complete giving of your body to your partner and this can only be done through agape which is self-sacrificing love. This can be seen as a powerful view of the importance of love in a sexual relationship because commitment has to be there. This commitment might not be at the same depth in relationships where there is no marriage and therefore less commitment.*

True, but where is this going?

An expansion but I really hope this is going to get on track soon.

Still a bit unclear as to where this is going.

Aha! Clever move and intro.

Followed by a good mix of information and evaluation. Maybe a bit confused at the start but got on track and would score well if the rest of the essay was like this.

The Bad

More traditional religious views of sex would argue that sex outside marriage has a bigger risk of being meaningless because there is not the same commitment that you would get in a marriage. This can be seen as a powerful view of the importance of love in a sexual relationship because commitment has to be there. This commitment might not be at the same depth in relationships where there is no marriage and therefore less commitment.

Basic statement.

This is too basic. There is a little evaluation but again, points needed to be 'worked.'

The Ugly

Religions are not against sexual relationships. Many religious people enjoy a full sex life with their partner so the first point is that religion is not against people having sex. The problem for religion is how it is used. In general, religions do not approve of sex outside marriage and consider that marriage is the only legal outlet for our sexual desires.

This is pure description which does not seem to be related to anything. No link is made to the question at all so it cannot get any marks.

Religion, Medicine and the Human Body

SQA Course Assessment Specification

Section 2: Morality and Belief

All learners should be able to:

- present in-depth factual and theoretical knowledge and understanding of the moral issues within each part.
- present detailed factual and theoretical knowledge and understanding of religious and non-religious viewpoints on different aspects of the moral issues in the part studied. These viewpoints will include: utilitarianism, religious authority.
- analyse the different aspects of the moral issues in the part studied.
- evaluate the religious and non-religious responses to different aspects of the moral issues in the part studied. Learners may answer questions in the context of a denomination or tradition within the religious responses.

Part D: Religion, Medicine and the Human Body

- Perspectives on life and death: sanctity of life, right to die
- Organ donation
- Assisted suicide
- Euthanasia and palliative care
- Status and treatment of embryos.

Analysis approaches

Issue: Perspectives on life and death: sanctity of life, right to die

Angles

- Reasons for religious and non-religious views on the sanctity of life
- Reasons for religious and non-religious views on the right to die
- Importance of the sanctity of life/right to die
- Consequences of the sanctity of life/right to die

- Moral issues raised by the sanctity of life/right to die
- Connection/tension between sanctity of life/right to die
- Relationship of sanctity of life/right to die to other aspects of the course.

You need to know (describe):

- religious and non-religious principles behind the sanctity of life/right to die
- medical positions on the sanctity of life/right to die
- the relationship of the sanctity of life/right to die to other aspects of the course.

You need to be able to explain (analyse):

- the reasons behind different views on the sanctity of life/right to die
- the connection between the sanctity of life/right to die and other aspects of the course
- similarities and differences between different approaches to sanctity of life/right to die
- the consequences of sanctity of life/right to die

You need to avoid:

- giving the impression that flushing the goldfish down the toilet is a form of euthanasia
- expressing points of view in analysis questions – even more tempting than missing RMPS Higher last two on a Friday so be warned
- confusing sanctity of life with the right to die.

You need to look out for:

- questions that look like analysis but are not
- the question stems that give you a clue about whether it is analysis or evaluation.

Question approaches

- Explain the conflict between the ideas of the right to die and the sanctity of life.
- Give an explanation of the moral implications of the right to die.
- Analyse religious responses to the sanctity of life.
- Explain the similarities and differences between religious and non-religious responses to the sanctity of life.
- What are the moral issues that are raised by the right to die?
- What reasons are sometimes given for defending the sanctity of life?
- Explain why the value of human life is such an important issue.
- What is the importance of understanding the reasons behind the principle of the right to die?
- Why is the right to die and the sanctity of life considered important in the moral debate surrounding medical ethics?
- Explain different views on the individual's rights over their own end-of-life decisions.

Issue: Organ donation

Angles

- Implications of opt-in/opt-out donation schemes
- Reasons behind opt-in/opt-out donation schemes
- Implications of using beating heart/non-beating heart/live donors
- Importance of organ donation in health care
- Implications of organ donation for the medical profession
- Consequences of the laws relating to organ donation
- Moral issues raised by organ donation
- Religious and non-religious views of organ donation
- Religious and non-religious views of the status of donors.

You need to know (describe):

- religious and non-religious views of organ donation
- the law and organ donation
- the types of donor
- the importance of organ donation
- the consequences of organ donation
- the moral issues raised by organ donation.

You need to be able to explain (analyse):

- the reasons behind different responses to organ donation
- the link between organ donation and patient autonomy
- similarities and differences between different approaches to different organ donation
- the consequences of using beating heart/non-beating heart/live donors
- the implications of different types of organ donation
- the moral issues raised by organ donation.

You need to avoid:

- offering to donate your brain – organs have to be living and healthy ...
- expressing points of view in analysis questions – very easy to do because organ donation is a highly controversial issue. Keep disciplined.
- mixing up the different organ donation schemes.

You need to look out for:

- questions that look like evaluation but are not
- the question stems that give you a clue about whether it is analysis or evaluation.

Question approaches

- Explain the reasons why organ donation can be a controversial issue.
- Give an explanation of the moral implications of one form of organ donation you have studied.
- Analyse religious responses to the status of organ donors.
- Explain the similarities and differences between religious and non-religious views on the morality of presumed consent.
- What are the moral issues that are raised by using beating heart donors?
- What reasons are sometimes given for objecting to organ donation?
- Explain why consent for organ donation raises moral issues.
- What is the importance of understanding the processes involved in organ donation?
- Why is organ donation a potentially controversial moral issue for some medical staff?
- Explain the reasons behind the desire to move from an opt-out to an opt-in system.

Issue: Assisted suicide

This is potentially a confusing bit of the course. The NHS website defines euthanasia and assisted suicide thus:

'**Euthanasia** is the act of deliberately ending a person's life to relieve suffering. **Assisted suicide** is the act of deliberately assisting or encouraging another person to kill themselves.'

See? So you have to be really careful with your definitions here and you need to be clear about what the difference is. Euthanasia is when you end someone's life deliberately and assisted suicide is when you help a person in one way or another to commit suicide. The problem is, of course, that physician-assisted suicide is a form of assisted suicide and it is quite possible that some people would describe it as euthanasia. So what do you do about this in an exam? If there is a specific question on it, make sure that very early on in your essay you understand exactly what it is that is being asked about and then work with that definition in mind.

Angles

- Reasons behind religious and non-religious views of assisted suicide
- Differences between assisted suicide and euthanasia
- Comparison of assisted suicide and euthanasia
- Moral issues raised by assisted suicide
- Connection between assisted suicide and the right to die
- Connection between assisted suicide and the sanctity of life.

You need to know (describe):

- religious and non-religious views of assisted suicide
- reasons behind religious and non-religious views of assisted suicide
- the moral issues raised by assisted suicide
- definitions of assisted suicide
- the law and assisted suicide.

You need to be able to explain (analyse):

- the reasons behind different responses to assisted suicide
- the link between assisted suicide and sanctity of life/right to die
- similarities and differences between different approaches to assisted suicide
- the consequences of assisted suicide
- the moral issues raised by assisted suicide
- the possible conflict between the sanctity of life and the right to die
- the moral difference between euthanasia and assisted suicide.

You need to avoid:

- arguing that lemmings are a good example of assisted suicide; they are not, they are really silly rodents who just don't get it
- expressing points of view in analysis questions – very easy to do because assisted suicide is a highly controversial issue.

You need to look out for:

- questions that look like analysis but are not
- the question stems that give you a clue about whether it is analysis or evaluation
- confusing assisted suicide with types of euthanasia.

Question approaches

- Explain ways in which assisted suicide can be justified.
- Give an explanation of the moral implications of assisted suicide.
- Analyse religious responses to assisted suicide.
- Explain the similarities and differences between religious and non-religious views on assisted suicide.
- What are the moral issues that are raised for those who assist a person to commit suicide?
- What reasons are behind non-religious views that support assisted suicide?
- Explain why there is a moral debate about assisted suicide.
- Give an analysis of the implications of assisted suicide.
- Why is the right to die considered important in the moral debate surrounding assisted suicide?
- Explain the reasons behind the desire to give individuals control over their death.

Issue: Euthanasia and palliative care

Angles

- Reasons behind religious and non-religious views of euthanasia/palliative care
- Differences between assisted suicide and euthanasia
- Comparison of assisted suicide and euthanasia
- Moral issues raised by different types of euthanasia/palliative care
- Connection between euthanasia/palliative care and the right to die
- Connection between euthanasia/palliative care and the sanctity of life.

You need to know (describe):

- religious and non-religious views of euthanasia/palliative care
- reasons behind religious and non-religious views of euthanasia/palliative care
- the moral issues raised by euthanasia/palliative care
- methods and types of euthanasia
- the law and euthanasia
- principles behind palliative care.

You need to be able to explain (analyse):

- the reasons behind different responses to euthanasia/palliative care
- the link between euthanasia/palliative care and sanctity of life/right to die
- similarities and differences between different approaches to euthanasia/palliative care
- the consequences of euthanasia/palliative care
- the moral issues raised by euthanasia/palliative care
- the possible conflict between the sanctity of life and the right to die
- the moral difference between euthanasia and assisted suicide.

You need to avoid:

- expressing points of view in analysis questions
- confusing different types of euthanasia
- pretending to be dead during the exam – not a mark earner.

You need to look out for:

- questions that look like analysis but are not
- the question stems that give you a clue about whether it is analysis or evaluation
- questions on different types of euthanasia.

Question approaches

- Explain ways in which euthanasia can be justified.
- Give an explanation of the moral implications of palliative care.

- Analyse religious responses to euthanasia.
- Explain the similarities and differences between religious and non-religious views on voluntary euthanasia.
- What are the moral issues that are raised by palliative care?
- What reasons are behind non-religious views that support palliative care?
- Explain why there is a moral debate about euthanasia.
- Give an analysis of the implications of palliative care.
- Why is the right to die considered important in the moral debate surrounding euthanasia?

Issue: Status and treatment of embryos

Angles

- Reasons behind religious and non-religious views of the status of embryos
- Differences between different viewpoints on the treatment of embryos
- Comparison of the moral issues arising from different treatments of embryos
- Moral issues raised by different definitions of life/uses of embryos
- Connection between the status of embryos and the sanctity of life
- Connection between viewpoints of the status of embryos and the use of embryos.

You need to know (describe):

- religious and non-religious views of the status and treatment of embryos
- reasons behind religious and non-religious views on the status and treatment of embryos
- definitions of life
- different treatments of embryos
- relationship between the principles of the sanctity of life and the treatment and status of embryos.

You need to be able to explain (analyse):

- the reasons behind treatment of embryos
- the link between the right to life and the treatment and status of embryos
- similarities and differences between different approaches to the status of embryos/ treatment of embryos
- the consequences of different perceptions on the beginning of life/treatment of embryos
- the moral issues raised by the treatment of embryos
- the possible conflict between the sanctity of life and the use of embryos
- the moral difference between different uses of embryos.

You need to avoid:

- expressing points of view in analysis questions
- confusing the status of embryos with the use of embryos.

You need to look out for:

- questions that look like analysis but are not
- the question stems that give you a clue about whether it is analysis or evaluation
- questions on specific types of embryo use.

Question approaches

- Explain ways in which the use of embryos for research purposes can be justified.
- Give an explanation of the moral implications of one use of an embryo that you have studied.
- Analyse religious responses to the status of embryos.
- Explain the similarities and differences between religious and non-religious views on the treatment of embryos.
- What are the moral issues that are raised by IVF?
- What reasons are behind non-religious views that prohibit the use of embryos for research?
- Explain why there is a moral debate about the status/treatment of embryos.
- Give an analysis of the implications of different types of embryo use.
- Why is the sanctity of life considered important in the moral debate surrounding embryos?

Evaluation approaches

Just like in World Religions, evaluation questions lend themselves best to having a statement followed by a question. Like in World Religions we have a change of approach here. There will be a number of statements listed below. In most cases issues and responses will be interchangeable. Just adapt them as you wish. Following the statements there will be the standard 'to what extent' or 'how far do you agree' type questions which can be attached to any of the statements.

Issue: Right to die and sanctity of life

Angles

- Right to die and end of life decisions
- Sanctity of life and end of life decisions
- Sanctity of life and the treatment/use of embryos
- Relationship between the principles of the right to die and the sanctity of life.

You need to know (describe):

- religious and non-religious principles behind the sanctity of life/right to die
- medical positions on the sanctity of life/right to die
- the relationship of the sanctity of life/right to die to other aspects of the course.

You need to be able to comment on (evaluate):

- the moral issues raised by the sanctity of life/right to die in general
- the moral issues raised by the sanctity of life/right to die in each of the other issues covered in the course
- the moral issues raised by responses to the sanctity of life/right to die
- the relevance of religious/non-religious views on the sanctity of life/right to die
- the consequences of different views on sanctity of life/right to die.

You need to avoid:

- confusing the two. They are closely related so if a question is about one of them make sure you stay with it.
- thinking that it is only opinions that are wanted here; religious concerns can be shown by the responses they have.

You need to look out for:

- questions that ask you for a discussion of one or the other. Make sure you can write in detail about both of them.
- questions that ask you to relate either of them to a specific issue in the course.

Question approaches
Statements

- 'The sanctity of life is more important than the right to die.'
- 'The sanctity of life is an out-dated idea.'
- 'Upholding the sanctity of life creates more suffering than good.'
- 'Nature should be allowed to take its course in medical decision-making.'
- 'Teachings on the sanctity of life are contradictory.'
- 'A person's right to die is an inviolable right.'
- 'Decisions about the right to die and the sanctity of life should be done on a case-by-case basis.'
- 'The right to die is one of the most dangerous rights for anyone to have.'
- 'God has complete sovereignty over life and death.'
- 'The sanctity of life and the right to die are mutually exclusive.'

Statement question stems

- To what extent do you agree?
- How far do you agree?
- Is this statement fair?
- To what extent might non-religious and religious people agree?
- How successfully can religious people support this view?
- To what extent might this view be supported?
- Evaluate this statement.
- Discuss.

- How relevant is this view?
- To what extent is this important in the debate about the sanctity of life/right to die?

Direct questions

- Why should the right to die be a concern for religious people?
- To what extent do modern medical advances complicate matters in relation to the right to die?
- How far do you agree that there should be absolute rules about the sanctity of life?
- How effective are religious responses to the right to die?
- To what extent are non-religious responses to the sanctity of life morally acceptable?
- Do you agree that doctors should not be allowed to 'play God'?
- Why should the right to die be a moral concern for everyone?
- Why do some people consider religious views on the sanctity of life to be out-dated?
- To what extent should society be concerned by issues relating to the preservation of life?
- How far do you agree that religion needs to get over its obsession with the sanctity of life?
- Has religion got anything meaningful to contribute to the debate about the right to die?

Issue: Organ donation

Angles

- Views on organ donation
- Views on each type of organ donor
- Moral issues raised by types of organ donor/system of donation/role of medical staff
- Approaches to organ donation
- Morality of presumed consent/beating heart donors/non-beating heart donors/live donors
- Medical profession and organ donation
- Patient autonomy and organ donation.

You need to know (describe):

- the different types of organ donation systems
- non-religious/religious views on the different systems of organ donation
- the good/bad points about their views
- criticisms/support of their views
- relationship between organ donation and the right to life/sanctity of life
- different types of organ donor
- definitions of death.

You need to be able to comment on (evaluate):

- the moral issues raised by organ donation
- the moral issues raised by responses to organ donation
- the relevance of religious/non-religious views on organ donation
- the importance of the donor in the debate about organ donation
- ethical issues raised for medical staff.

You need to avoid:

- anonymously leaving your Yamaha CP40 (with power adapter and free 'teach yourself' book) at the casualty department at Perth Royal Infirmary as your organ donation
- spending too much time on organ distribution and allocation in answers – the issue is donation, not the other two.

You need to look out for:

- questions that ask you to compare religious and non-religious responses
- questions that focus only on one type of donor (unlikely but possible)
- questions that ask why organ donation could be morally wrong
- questions that focus on one type of donor consent.

Question approaches
Statements

- 'Using organs from live donors is morally wrong.'
- ' Everyone has a duty to make their organs available for donation.'
- 'The only acceptable type of donor is a non-beating heart donor.'
- 'Donating your organs is the ultimate act of charity.'
- 'People who do not donate should not be allowed to receive.'
- 'Presumed consent is a violation of human rights.'
- 'Organ donation is an act of love for fellow human beings. There are no moral issues with it.'
- 'Since no-one can agree on a definition of death, organs should not be donated by anyone.'
- 'The moral implications of live donations are so great that they should never be done.'

Statement question stems

- To what extent do you agree?
- How far do you agree?
- Is this statement fair?
- To what extent might non-religious and religious people agree?
- How successfully can religious people support this view?
- To what extent might this view be supported?
- Evaluate this statement.
- Discuss.

- How relevant is this view?
- To what extent is this important in the debate about organ donation?

Direct questions

- Why do many religious people consider organ donation to be a duty?
- To what extent is there agreement in the medical profession about the morality of organ donation?
- Why are opt out systems of organ donation controversial?
- Why might some religious people not support organ donation of any kind?
- Why do some non-religious people object to the use of living donors?
- Discuss the weaknesses, identified by some, of religious views on organ donation.
- To what extent are non-religious arguments in favour of opt out donation systems persuasive?
- Evaluate the arguments for and against opt in donation systems.
- To what extent are religious views on organ donation relevant today?
- How far do you agree that the sanctity of life is the key moral issue in the debate about organ donation?
- To what extent is the use of beating heart donors morally wrong?
- Has religion got anything to contribute to the debate about organ donation?

Issue: Assisted suicide and euthanasia

Angles

- Views on assisted suicide/euthanasia
- Views on each type of euthanasia
- Moral differences between each different type of euthanasia
- Approaches to legalising euthanasia
- Morality of assisted suicide
- Medical profession and end of life decisions.

You need to know (describe):

- the different types and methods of euthanasia including double effect
- secular/religious views on the different types and methods of euthanasia
- the good/bad points about their responses
- criticisms/support of their positions
- relationship between assisted suicide/euthanasia.

You need to be able to comment on (evaluate):

- the moral issues raised by euthanasia and assisted suicide
- the moral issues raised by responses to euthanasia and assisted suicide
- the relevance of religious/non-religion views on euthanasia and assisted suicide
- the importance of the right to die and the sanctity of life in the moral debate surrounding euthanasia and assisted suicide.

You need to avoid:

- saying that religions support euthanasia because they accept double effect – that is not how religions see it as a whole.

You need to look out for:

- questions that ask you to compare religious and secular responses
- questions that focus only on one type or method of euthanasia
- questions that ask why religious people might support euthanasia.

Question approaches
Statements

- 'Non-voluntary euthanasia is killing the defenceless.'
- 'Double effect is nothing but euthanasia by the back door.'
- 'A right that is more important than the right to life is the right not to be killed – euthanasia denies people that right.'
- 'How can anyone in this day and age justify continuing the suffering of someone who does not want to live?'
- 'God gives life and only God can take it away.'
- 'Religious support for double effect is effectively support for euthanasia.'
- 'Assisted suicide is the only morally acceptable form of taking one's own life.'
- 'Assisted suicide respects the sanctity of life and the right to die at the same time.'
- 'Killing is worse than letting die.'
- 'A compassionate society should respect the individual's right to die/sanctity of life.'

Statement question stems

- To what extent do you agree?
- How far do you agree?
- Is this statement fair?
- To what extent might non-religious and religious people agree?
- How successfully can religious people support this view?
- To what extent might this view be supported?
- Evaluate this statement.
- Discuss.
- How relevant is this view?
- To what extent is this important in the debate about euthanasia/assisted suicide?

Direct questions

- Why do religious people consider double effect to be morally acceptable but euthanasia to be wrong?
- Should the medical professionals have any position at all on euthanasia?
- Why is non-voluntary euthanasia considered to be more of a problem by some people than voluntary euthanasia?

- Why might some religious people support voluntary euthanasia?
- Why do some religious people object to arguments supporting euthanasia?
- Discuss the weaknesses, identified by some, of religious views on assisted suicide.
- To what extent are non-religious arguments in favour of euthanasia persuasive?
- Evaluate the arguments for and against voluntary euthanasia.
- Why should assisted suicide be a concern for religious people?
- To what extent is the legalisation of voluntary euthanasia morally correct?
- How far do you agree that the individual's rights come before any other considerations in decisions about end of life care?
- To what extent is assisted suicide morally wrong?
- Has religion got anything to contribute to the debate about euthanasia?

Issue: Palliative care

Angles

- Palliative care as an alternative to euthanasia
- Palliative care as a concern for society/religion
- Moral issues arising from palliative care
- Religious and non-religious responses to palliative care
- Relationship between palliative care and sanctity of life/right to die.

You need to know (describe):

- the nature and purpose of palliative care
- the moral arguments surrounding palliative care
- arguments for/against palliative care
- religious/non-religious responses to palliative care.

You need to be able to comment on (evaluate):

- the moral issues raised by palliative care
- the moral issues raised by responses to palliative care
- the relevance of religious/non-religious views on palliative care
- the importance of the right to die and the sanctity of life in the moral debate surrounding palliative care
- palliative care as an alternative to euthanasia/assisted suicide.

You need to avoid:

- straying into discussions about euthanasia when the question is clearly about palliative care alone – very easy to fall into this trap because there is probably more to say about euthanasia than palliative care.

You need to look out for:

- questions that focus purely on palliative care
- questions that ask for a religious view – your answer will contain loads of secular insights which are shared with religious people but, if you can, find a couple of things that are clearly religious
- questions that link palliative care to the sanctity of life principle.

Question approaches
Statements

- 'Palliative care is the mark of a compassionate society.'
- 'The only moral alternative to euthanasia is palliative care.'
- 'Palliative care is a positive end of life decision. Euthanasia is negative in every way.'
- 'Everyone should support palliative care as an alternative to euthanasia.'
- 'Care of the dying should focus on making euthanasia unnecessary.'
- 'Palliative care promotes the sanctity of life.'
- 'The right to die should be replaced by the right to have quality palliative care.'
- 'Palliative care is costly and has few benefits for society as a whole.'

Statement question stems

- To what extent do you agree?
- How far do you agree?
- Is this statement fair?
- To what extent might non-religious and religious people agree?
- How successfully can religious people support this view?
- To what extent might this view be supported?
- Evaluate this statement.
- Discuss.
- How relevant is this view?
- To what extent is this important in the debate about palliative care?

Direct questions

- To what extent is palliative care beneficial to society?
- Why is palliative care sometimes considered to be a luxury we cannot afford?
- Why should palliative care be a concern for religious people?
- Why do some religious people argue that palliative care is the only alternative to euthanasia?
- To what extent should religious people support palliative care?
- To what extent should palliative care be a concern of religion?
- Discuss the views of at least one non-religious response you have studied to palliative care.
- Do you agree that palliative care may sometimes not be a compassionate way to treat the dying?

Issue: Status/treatment of embryos

Angles

- The moral status of the embryo
- The sanctity of life and the embryo
- The implications of different views on the status of the embryo
- Religious and non-religious views of the embryo
- The morality of different uses of embryos.

You need to know (describe):

- religious and non-religious views of the status and treatment of embryos
- reasons behind religious and non-religious views on the status and treatment of embryos
- definitions of life
- different treatments of embryos
- relationship between the principles of the sanctity of life and the treatment and status of embryos.

You need to be able to comment on (evaluate):

- the moral issues raised by status and treatment of embryos
- the moral issues raised by responses to the status and treatment of embryos
- the relevance of religious/non-religious views on the status and treatment of embryos
- the importance of the sanctity of life in the moral debate surrounding the status of embryos
- various uses of embryos, e.g. stuff your teacher has covered which may include IVF, research, abortion.

You need to avoid:

- going off issue – embryo issues are very emotive and it is easy to lose sight of the question angle. Keep checking that you are writing relevant stuff.
- arguing that omelettes are made of aborted chicken embryos – 'tis true, check it out on Wikipedia (the source of all human knowledge).

You need to look out for:

- questions that link the status of the embryo with its treatment
- questions that focus on one particular aspect of the treatment of embryos
- questions that ask for a religious view – your answer will contain loads of secular insights which are shared with religious people but, if you can, find a couple of things that are clearly religious.
- questions that focus on one particular reason for using embryos
- questions about religious and secular reasons for NOT using the status/treatment of embryos.

Question approaches
Statements

- 'Religious views on the status of the embryo are unhelpful.'
- 'It's time we got over this love affair with the human embryo. It is not human. End of story.'
- 'The embryo deserves the benefit of the doubt.'
- 'God has willed every embryo to exist therefore nothing can be done to harm them.'
- 'Whatever way you look at it the embryo is a living thing and it is being harmed.'
- 'The embryo is a potential human. Nothing more and nothing less.'
- 'The benefits that arise from using embryos are so great that concerns about its status should be put to one side.'
- 'Using embryos for any purpose is inviting trouble.'
- 'The problem with using embryos is that science will always want to push the boundaries.'
- 'If embryo use is declared wrong then we have no need to worry about where it will go next.'
- 'We do not have the right to play God with embryos.'
- 'Using embryos is taking human power too far.'
- 'If embryo use is playing God, wouldn't God want to use embryos to save lives?'
- 'Slippery slopes are dangerous. You have no idea where you end up. That is why embryo use for any purpose is wrong.'
- 'Abortion is embryo abuse.'
- 'The key issue in the debate about the status of embryos is about how they can benefit humanity.'

Statement question stems

- To what extent do you agree?
- How far do you agree?
- Is this statement fair?
- To what extent might non-religious and religious people agree?
- How successfully can religious people support this view?
- To what extent might this view be supported?
- Evaluate this statement.
- Discuss.
- How relevant is this view?
- To what extent is this important in the debate about the status/use of embryos?

Direct questions

- Why might some religious people consider the embryo to be human?
- Why is the status of the embryo a moral issue?
- Why is the status of the embryo considered to be an important issue?
- Explain why some religious people can accept limited embryo use.
- Why do some people consider the embryo not to be human?
- How strong is the 'playing God' argument?

- To what extent is the 'slippery slope' argument against the use of embryos successful?
- To what extent do arguments about the use of embryos succeed?

Exemplar analysis points

Q Explain the reasons why religious people might object to euthanasia.

The Good

The reason they are against euthanasia is because God gives life and only God can take it away. It is not up to the state to decide who lives and who dies, this is a decision that only God can make.

Well done, at least a couple of marks here.

Another reason they would be unhappy about it is that it makes it legal to kill another person. They would say that euthanasia is killing, nothing else, just killing and in the Bible it says in the Ten Commandments that we should not kill.

And again!

Another reason is that the law gets us on a slippery slope. If we take away the right of people not to be killed then what next? Do we euthanize people because they are no longer useful and not just because they are in pain? This leads to legalising causing us to devalue human life.

Hat-trick of great ideas.

Just because we are suffering we should not think that the suffering is worthless nor should we think that our life is worthless. All of these things have value according to religious people.

Full house, great ideas.

The Bad

The reason they are against euthanasia is because God gives life and only God can take it away. Another reason they would be unhappy about it is that it makes it legal to kill another person. Another reason is that the law gets us on a slippery slope. This leads to legalising causing us to devalue human life. Just because we are suffering we should not think that the suffering is worthless. All of these things have value according to religious people.

It's a bit disjointed isn't it? You can see how none of the points have been expanded. This is a quick route to a C/D. Never going to get you close to an A.

The Ugly

The reason they are against euthanasia is because God gives life and only God can take it away. Euthanasia can never be right because it is too hard to stop people abusing it. Also it puts doctors under pressure and they take the hippopotamus oath which means that they cannot harm patients or kill them which is a good thing because I would not like my doctor to put me down.

> Evaluation – this is going nowhere.

> Yes, the hippo oath. Revered in medicine across the world.

Exemplar evaluation points

Q To what extent do you agree that interference with embryos is wrong?

The Good

IVF is one use of embryos. The status of the embryo is unclear. Some people see the embryo as a person, some a non-person and some a potential person. If you see the embryo as a person then it is clear that you are working with a human being which is the view of Pope John Paul II which is still the view of the Church today. If the embryo is a non-person then there is not really an issue because you are not dealing with a human being and if it is a potential person, very clear rules about what you can and cannot do are required so that the rights of the potential person are not infringed.

On balance there is no clear view on the status of the embryo. Perhaps the view that the embryo should be given the benefit of the doubt until we know for sure is the safest position. This view does not prevent any use at all of the embryo but at the same time prevents any abuse of the embryo.

A second issue relates to what can be done with the embryo. There are drawbacks of allowing scientists to do what they like because that could lead to the creation of monsters. There could be drawbacks related to creating saviour siblings which could be seen as exploiting an innocent person or allowing people to create designer babies rather than taking their chances. However, Robin Marantz Henig said it was similar to 'how people get used to all sorts of new technology ... at first it seems like it's abhorrent and it's something that we absolutely shouldn't do. And then for a while it seems kind of miraculous ... And then after a while, the technology just becomes part of the fabric of daily life.'

This answer would be well on its way to an A. Note the excellent mix of factual information and evaluation. There are views being expressed here, examples used to highlight points and judgements being made left, right and centre. Note also how the 'I' word has been avoided which means that this reads like quite an academic piece.

The Bad

One problem of IVF is that it is only successful one in three times which is why the NHS gives couples only three goes to have a baby. Another problem is designer babies because people should not be allowed to choose what baby they have because this makes the baby a product and not a human being. The bad side is that IVF might be killing a person.

If several points like this were made then it is unlikely that they would score more than a mark each time. This is because there is no depth to the points. This person has left the marker to work out his line of thought unlike the 'Good' essay where the person has written down how they worked out their point of view. Just stating your point of view is not enough. Like in Maths, you have got to show your working to get marks.

The Ugly

IVF has good points and bad points. Good points are that it lets childless couples have babies and let's face it everyone has the right to have a baby if they want to have one. Another good point is that saviour siblings can be made like in My Sister's Keeper.

Sloppy answer – looks like this person was in a rush to leave the exam room. This has very little KU in it and next to no evaluation. Take this approach with other points and the essay will be lucky if it scores more than just a couple of marks.

Religion and Conflict

SQA Course Assessment Specification

Section 2: Morality and Belief

All learners should be able to:

- present in-depth factual and theoretical knowledge and understanding of the moral issues within each part.
- present detailed factual and theoretical knowledge and understanding of religious and non-religious viewpoints on different aspects of the moral issues in the part studied. These viewpoints will include: utilitarianism, religious authority.
- analyse the different aspects of the moral issues in the part studied.
- evaluate the religious and non-religious responses to different aspects of the moral issues in the part studied. Learners may answer questions in the context of a denomination or tradition within the religious responses.

Part E: Religion and Conflict

- Causes and justifications for war
- Responses to conflict and alternatives to war
- Strategies of modern warfare
- Consequences of war.

Analysis approaches

Issues: Causes and justifications of war; Consequences of war

Angles

- Connection between causes and justifications of war
- Influence of religious teaching on the causes and justifications of war
- Reasons for religious and non-religious views of the causes of war
- Reasons for religious and non-religious views of the justifications of war
- Moral issues raised by the causes and justifications of war
- Responsibility for wars.

You need to know (describe):

- the causes of war and its justifications
- different religious and non-religious views and responses to the causes and justifications of war
- the moral issues raised by the causes and justifications of war.

You need to be able to explain (analyse):

- the reasons behind different responses to war and its justifications
- the link between different religious and non-religious views of war
- similarities and differences between different approaches to the causes and justifications of war
- how the causes and justifications of war are related to other aspects of Religion and Conflict
- the consequences of different causes and justifications of war
- the use of the word 'aggression' or term 'acts of aggression' – they have a wider meaning than war.

You need to avoid:

- declaring war on Dumfries and Galloway at any time, especially on a Sunday when there's not many buses
- expressing points of view in analysis questions – even more tempting than missing RMPS Higher last two on a Friday so be warned.

You need to look out for:

- questions that look like analysis but are not
- the question stems that give you a clue about whether it is analysis or evaluation.

Question approaches

- Explain the connection between the justification of war and the causes of war.
- Give an explanation of the moral implications of the consequences of war.
- Analyse religious responses to the impact of war on society.
- Explain the similarities and differences between religious and non-religious responses to the causes of war.
- What are the moral issues that are raised by the justifications of war?
- What reasons are sometimes used to support the grave consequences of war?
- Explain why the causes of war raise moral issues.
- What is the importance of understanding the causes of war?
- Why are the consequences of war considered important in the moral debate surrounding conflict?
- Explain different views on war as a form of peace-making.

Issues: Responses to conflict and alternatives to war; Consequences of war

Angles

- Connection between the consequences of war and moral responses to it
- Influence of religious teaching on the alternatives to war
- Reasons for religious and non-religious responses to war
- Reasons for religious and non-religious responses to alternatives to war
- Reasons for religious and non-religious views of war
- Moral issues raised by the alternatives to war
- Responsibility to find alternatives to war.

You need to know (describe):

- different responses to conflict, e.g. retaliation, surrender, ultimatum, protest
- different alternatives to war, e.g. pacifism, diplomacy, sanctions
- different religious and non-religious views and responses to the alternatives to war
- the moral issues raised by the alternatives to war.

You need to be able to explain (analyse):

- the reasons behind different responses to war
- the reasons behind different responses to the alternatives to war
- the link between different religious and non-religious views of responses to war and its alternatives
- similarities and differences between different approaches to the responses and alternatives to war
- how the responses and alternatives to war are related to other aspects of Religion and Conflict
- the consequences of alternatives to war.

You need to avoid:

- imposing economic sanctions on the dinner ladies because the portions are too wee
- expressing points of view in analysis questions.

You need to look out for:

- questions that look like analysis but are not
- the question stems that give you a clue about whether it is analysis or evaluation
- specific mentions of things like pacifism.

Question approaches

- Explain the connection between the alternatives to war and the consequences of war.
- Give an explanation of the moral implications of retaliation after being attacked.
- Analyse religious responses to the alternatives to war.
- Explain the similarities and differences between religious and non-religious responses to pacifism.
- What are the moral issues that are raised by self-defence?
- What reasons are sometimes used to argue against sanctions?
- Explain why some people view military action as the only response to an attack.
- What is the importance of understanding the alternatives to war?
- Why are the alternatives to war considered important in the moral debate surrounding conflict?
- Explain different views on war as a form of peace-making.

Issue: Strategies of modern warfare; Consequences of war

Angles

- Connection between the consequences of war and strategies of modern warfare
- Influence of religious teaching on modern strategies of war
- Reasons for religious and non-religious responses to modern strategies of war
- Consequences of war
- Morality of defence and deterrence strategies in modern warfare
- Moral issues raised by new technology and warfare.

You need to know (describe):

- different strategies of modern warfare, e.g. sanctions, diplomacy, WMD, terror, social media
- different purposes of modern warfare
- different religious and non-religious views and responses to modern strategies
- the moral issues raised by the methods of modern strategies of war
- the role of deterrence and defence in modern strategies of war.

You need to be able to explain (analyse):

- the reasons behind different types of modern strategies
- the reasons behind different responses to modern strategies
- the link between different religious and non-religious views of modern strategies
- similarities and differences between different approaches to modern strategies
- the consequences of modern strategies of war
- how the modern strategies of war are related to other aspects of Religion and Conflict
- the role of defence and deterrence in modern strategies.

You need to avoid:

- expressing points of view in analysis questions.

You need to look out for:

- questions that look like analysis but are not
- the question stems that give you a clue about whether it is analysis or evaluation
- specific mentions of things like weapons of mass destruction or general themes likes deterrence.

Question approaches

- Explain the connection between modern strategies of war and the consequences of war.
- Give an explanation of the moral implications of the use of smart weapons.
- Analyse religious responses to deterrence as a strategy of modern warfare.
- Explain the similarities and differences between religious and non-religious responses to weapons of mass destruction.
- What are the moral issues that are raised by targeting civilians?
- What reasons are sometimes used to support attacks on the civilian population?
- Explain why some people view weapons of mass destruction as morally right.
- Explain the importance of deterrence in the debate about modern strategies of war?
- Why are the consequences of using weapons of mass destruction considered important in the moral debate surrounding conflict?
- Explain different views on possession of hi-tech weapons as a means to keeping the peace.

Evaluation approaches

Just like in World Religions, evaluation questions lend themselves best to having a statement followed by a question. Like in World Religions we have a change of approach here. There will be a number of statements listed below. In most cases issues and responses will be interchangeable. Just adapt them as you wish. Following the statements there will be the standard 'to what extent' or 'how far do you agree' type questions which can be attached to any of the statements.

Issue: Causes and justifications of war; Consequences of war

Angles

- Morality of different causes/justifications/consequences of war
- Moral issues raised by not going to war
- Moral issues raised by conflict in general

- Effectiveness of war in settling international disputes
- Causes/justifications/consequences as a concern for religious people.

You need to know (describe):

- the causes of war and its justifications
- different religious and non-religious views and responses to the causes and justifications of war
- the moral issues raised by the causes and justifications of war.

You need to be able to comment on (evaluate):

- the moral issues raised by the causes of war
- the moral issues raised by justifications of war
- the relevance of religious/non-religious views on the causes of war
- the importance of the causes/justifications/consequences of war in the moral debate surrounding conflict
- the extent to which the cost of war is justified.

You need to avoid:

- watching the *Lord of the Rings* trilogy because the Council of Elrond could have done a bit more to prevent the war
- thinking that it is only opinions that are wanted here; religious concerns can be shown by the responses they have.

You need to look out for:

- questions that ask you for a discussion of one particular cause (unlikely but a possibility for a main cause)
- questions that ask for a religious view – your answer will contain loads of secular insights which are shared with religious people but, if you can, find a couple of things that are clearly religious.

Question approaches
Statements

- 'No causes of war are justifiable.'
- 'War is only right as a last resort.'
- 'The causes of war are a concern for everyone.'
- 'The consequences of war are so significant that no war can be justified.'
- 'Religious responses to war are weak and ineffective.'
- 'Wars are necessary.'
- 'Without the threat of war nobody is safe.'
- 'The only effective response to the causes of war is to get tough on rogue leaders.'
- 'Responses to the causes of war tend to be all talk and no action.'

- 'The consequences of not fighting a war are more important than the consequences when you fight a war.'
- 'Self-defence is the only morally justifiable cause of war.'

Statement question stems

- To what extent do you agree?
- How far do you agree?
- Is this statement fair?
- To what extent might non-religious and religious people agree?
- How successfully can religious people support this view?
- To what extent might this view be supported?
- Evaluate this statement.
- Discuss.
- How relevant is this view?
- To what extent is this important in the debate about the causes of war?

Direct questions

- Why should the causes of war be a concern for religious people?
- To what extent is everyone to blame for war in one way or another?
- How far do you agree that the consequences of war should be considered before deciding on declaring war?
- How effective are religious responses to the causes of war?
- To what extent are non-religious responses to the causes of war successful?
- Do you agree that responses to the causes of war have limited success?
- Why should the justifications of war be a moral concern?
- Why do some people consider war to be wrong in all circumstances?
- To what extent should war be used to defend freedom and democracy?
- How far do you agree that war is motivated mainly by greed?
- Has religion got anything to contribute to the debate about the causes of war?

Issue: Responses to conflict and alternatives to war; Consequences of war

Angles

- Morality of different responses and alternatives to war
- Moral issues raised by not going to war
- Moral issues raised by conflict in general
- Effectiveness of alternatives to war
- Responses/alternatives/consequences of war as a concern for religious people.

You need to know (describe):

- different alternatives to war
- different religious and non-religious views and responses to alternatives to war
- the moral issues raised by the alternatives to war
- the moral issues raised by the consequences of alternatives to war
- the role of possession and deterrence in the debate about alternatives to war
- the impact of modern technology on alternatives to war.

You need to be able to comment on (evaluate):

- the moral issues raised by the responses to conflict
- the moral issues raised by alternatives to war
- the relevance of religious/non-religious views on the responses to conflict/alternatives to war
- the importance of the alternatives to war in the moral debate surrounding conflict
- the extent to which alternatives to war are justified.

You need to avoid:

- camouflaging yourself in the exam; they will find you
- thinking that it is only opinions that are wanted here; religious concerns can be shown by the responses they have.

You need to look out for:

- questions that ask you for a discussion of one particular alternative (unlikely but a possibility for a main alternative)
- questions that ask for a religious view – your answer will contain loads of secular insights which are shared with religious people but, if you can, find a couple of things that are clearly religious.

Question approaches
Statements

- 'Pacifism is the only morally justifiable response to war.'
- 'There is no alternative to war that is without its moral problems too.'
- 'The responses to war are a concern for everyone.'
- 'The consequences of war are so significant that no war can be justified.'
- 'Religious responses to war are weak and ineffective.'
- 'Wars are necessary.'
- 'Without the threat of war nobody is safe.'
- 'The only effective response to war is to get tough on rogue leaders.'
- 'Alternatives to wars tend to be all talk and no action.'
- 'War has kept world peace not non-violence.'
- 'Economic sanctions as an alternative to war are more immoral than military action.'

Statement question stems

- To what extent do you agree?
- How far do you agree?
- Is this statement fair?
- To what extent might non-religious and religious people agree?
- How successfully can religious people support this view?
- To what extent might this view be supported?
- Evaluate this statement.
- Discuss.
- How relevant is this view?
- To what extent is this important in the debate about the alternatives to war?

Direct questions

- Why should the alternatives to war be a concern for religious people?
- To what extent would it be right for a religious person to support war?
- How far do you agree that alternatives to war are just wars under another name?
- How effective are religious responses to the consequences of war?
- To what extent can the alternatives to war be supported by religious and non-religious people?
- Do you agree that all alternatives to war have limited success?
- Why should pacifism be a moral concern?
- Why do some people consider war to be wrong in all circumstances?
- To what extent should war be used to defend freedom and democracy?
- How far do you agree that pacifism is motivated mainly by cowardice?
- Has religion got anything to contribute to the debate about responses to war?

Issue: Modern strategies of war; Consequences of war

Angles

- Connection between the consequences of war and strategies of modern warfare
- Influence of religious teaching on modern strategies of war
- Reasons for religious and non-religious responses to modern strategies of war
- Morality of defence and deterrence strategies in modern warfare
- Moral issues raised by new technology and warfare.

You need to know (describe):

- different strategies of modern warfare, e.g. sanctions, diplomacy, WMD, terror, social media
- different purposes of modern warfare
- different religious and non-religious views and responses to modern strategies
- the moral issues raised by the methods of modern strategies of war
- the role of deterrence and defence in modern strategies of war.

You need to be able to comment on (evaluate):

- the moral issues raised by the strategies of modern warfare
- the moral issues raised by smart weapons, hi-tech and social media in warfare
- the moral issues raised by WMD
- the morality of deterrence and possession
- the relevance of religious/non-religious views on the responses to strategies of modern warfare including the possibility of responses to specific types of weapon
- the importance of the alternatives to war in the moral debate surrounding modern strategies of warfare
- the extent to which modern strategies of war have impacted on debates about the morality of war.

You need to avoid:

- thinking that it is only opinions that are wanted here; religious concerns can be shown by the responses they have.

You need to look out for:

- questions that ask you for a discussion of one particular strategy (unlikely but a possibility for a main strategy)
- questions that ask for a religious view – your answer will contain loads of secular insights which are shared with religious people but, if you can, find a couple of things that are clearly religious.

Question approaches
Statements

- 'The use of smart weapons can be morally justified.'
- 'Weapons of mass destruction should be neither possessed nor used.'
- 'Deterrence contains intent and the intention is morally wrong.'
- 'The consequences of war are so significant that no war can now be justified.'
- 'Religious responses to different strategies used in modern warfare are weak and ineffective.'
- 'The loss of civilian life is necessary in war.'
- 'Without the threat of war nobody is safe.'
- 'The only effective response to aggression is the possession of weapons of mass destruction.'
- 'We cannot un-invent weapons of mass destruction so we should use them to maintain peace.'
- 'Weapons of mass destruction have kept world peace, not any other alternatives to war.'
- 'Economic sanctions as an alternative to war are more immoral than using weapons of mass destruction as a deterrent.'

Statement question stems

- To what extent do you agree?
- How far do you agree?
- Is this statement fair?
- To what extent might non-religious and religious people agree?
- How successfully can religious people support this view?
- To what extent might this view be supported?
- Evaluate this statement.
- Discuss.
- How relevant is this view?
- To what extent is this important in the debate about the strategies of modern warfare?

Direct questions

- Why should chemical and biological weapons be a concern for religious people?
- To what extent would it be right for a religious person to support deterrence?
- How far do you agree that the use of drones is immoral?
- How effective are religious responses to modern strategies of war?
- To what extent can pre-emptive strikes be morally justified?
- Do you agree that all modern strategies of war are morally wrong?
- Why should the methods used to secure peace be a moral concern?
- Why do some people consider war to be wrong in all circumstances?
- To what extent should war be used to defend freedom and democracy?

Exemplar analysis points

Q Explain how one moral perspective you have studied might be applied to issues arising from conflict.

The Good

One moral perspective I studied was religious authority. This is a normative ethical theory which can be applied to different moral issues. Religious authority is based on what sacred books like the Bible say or what famous writers or leaders have said. In the Bible it says that you should not kill. This was a problem for Christians because the Church was often involved in wars. They needed to find a way round this problem so the church developed ways of justifying them. Behind their just war theory were several ideas: the first was that it is wrong to take the lives

Good KU which nicely sets up the analysis to follow.

of people, secondly, that it was wrong to start a war and thirdly that there are times when countries must defend their people and defend what they think to be right.

> Good phrase to use – 'the reasons behind' because it shows that you can pick out different themes in the beliefs so you are pulling ideas together.

These ideas were then found in the rules that they developed for wars. For example, Just War comes under two headings, Jus ad Bellum and Jus in Bello which is fighting wars for the right reasons and in the right way. These two things are detailed and take into account the protection of innocent life. For example...

> Now themes have been identified and the candidate is going to go on and give examples. Good plan. Heading for an A.

The Bad

One moral perspective I studied was religious authority. In the Bible it says that you should not kill. This was a problem for Christians because the Church was often involved in wars. Behind their just war theory were several ideas: do not kill, defend yourself and fight fair. The Church then applied these rules in every war that they fought so they were not involved in unjust wars.

> Basic summary but it would get credit.

> Eh, nope. Jibberish. Go read a *Horrible History*.

The Ugly

In the Bible it says you should not kill. Christians have caused most wars in history so they are out of order for giving other people into trouble for fighting wars when they fight them themselves and go against the Bible

> Whit? A wee rant here. Somebody got out the wrong side of bed this morning.

Exemplar evaluation points

Q 'Winning a war is more important than worrying about the methods used to win it.' How far do you agree?

The Good

... Another concern about this view is that it allows all kinds of indiscriminate killing. Winning a war regardless of methods opens the door to all kinds of crimes against humanity. For example, it is known that war crimes are regularly committed by armed forces on the winning side and the culprits brought to justice. The fact that this is done shows that the methods used to win wars are important. You don't have to go back that far to see the American use of nuclear bombs in 1945 where civilians were targeted. The killing of non-combatants as a method of winning the war is wrong on so many grounds. However the long term result was that the war ended and no more people died. When the Enigma code was broken the British government had to pick and choose what German attacks were permitted because if all attacks were foiled the Germans would have known the code had been cracked. This shows that to win wars very difficult decisions have to be made and sometimes there has to be tough love which is almost utilitarian- the sacrifice of a few to save the many.

> Predicting the implications, and backing it up with a live example. Good move!

The Bad

... Another concern about this view is that it allows all kinds of indiscriminate killing. This can be seen in the use of chemical weapons in the Vietnam War. Civilians were legitimate targets in the American use of nuclear bombs in 1945.

> This is undeveloped. What would happen here is that the candidate would soon run out of things to say because he has to make loads of small points to build up marks rather than fewer points with more detail.

The Ugly

All types of war and violence are wrong. People die. End of story. It is never right. There are no excuses. It is just wrong even if it was against the Nazis or Saddam Hussein because they were just bad people and Hussein should have hanged and it is a pity that Hitler and co were not caught and given an unbelievably painful torture and then death.

> What is this about? Looks like someone is winging it here and been caught out.

Religious and Philosophical Questions

This section of the paper has four possible topics. You need to be very careful that you do not get the topics mixed up, especially 'Origins' and 'The Existence of God'. These topics could have questions that look similar but don't let that fool you. Different information is being sought in the different questions.

The RPQ questions will always be worth 20 marks and have both analysis and evaluation in them, along with the usual dose of KU. This means that you need to know detailed facts about the issue, be able to know what the story is behind them and then be able to pass some kind of comment or judgement on them. In theory the split is 12 for KU, 5 for Analysis and 5 for Evaluation but don't worry yourself about the marks distribution. Write it like a discursive essay and you will be fine. Let the marker worry about how the marks are divvied up.

The exemplars have to be set out in a different way because the analysis and evaluation is combined in the question and, of course, in the answer. The potential content of this unit is huge in its range so questions have to be quite general in nature. This is how the chapters relating to the RPQs have been set out:

- SQA Course Specification
- Issue
- Angles
- You need to know
- You need to be able to explain
- You need to be able to comment on
- You need to avoid
- You need to look out for
- Statements
- Statement question stems
- Direct questions

You should mix and match the questions because in the exam they can be about specific issues or they can be questions that cut across several issues. Once again, this is an excellent activity for an RMPS Higher party or maybe even the RMPS study weekend that Mrs McGillivray organised to Arbroath.

Origins

SQA Course Assessment Specification

Section 3: Religious and Philosophical Questions

The content in each Part describes ideas and arguments which may feature in both religious and non-religious responses.

Part A: Origins

- Role of a creator
- Distinction between literal and metaphorical interpretations of creation accounts
- Scientific theories: the Big Bang and evolution
- Perspectives on the compatibility between reason and faith.

Issue: Role of a creator

Angles

- Nature of the creator as revealed by the creation
- Involvement of the creator in creation
- Purpose of the creation for the creator
- Evidence of a creator
- Strengths and weaknesses of belief in a creator.

You need to know (describe):

- different religious views of what the creator might be like
- different religious views on the role of the creator in creation
- different religious views on the purpose of creation
- different religious views on how the origins of life support belief in creation.

You need to be able to explain (analyse):

- the ideas behind different religious views of the creator
- the ideas behind different understandings of the creator's role in creation

- the ideas behind different understandings of the purpose of creation
- the ideas behind different religious views on how God's existence may be proved by creation
- the reasons behind religious and non-religious criticisms of ideas relating to the role of the creator
- similarities and differences between religious and non-religious views on the role of the creator
- the implications of religious and non-religious views on the role of the creator
- strengths and weaknesses of belief in a creator.

You need to be able to comment on (evaluate):

- the strengths and weaknesses of religious and non-religious views on the role of the creator
- how sound the religious and non-religious views on the role of the creator are
- the relevance of religious and non-religious views on the role of the creator
- various issues identified by the questions (useless advice but true nonetheless).

You need to avoid:

- giving the impression that all religious people believe the same about the role of the creator
- giving the impression that science and religion are always in conflict.

You need to look out for:

- questions that ask why religious people might disagree about the role of the creator in creation.

Question approaches
Statements

- 'Science can support the view that there is a creator.'
- 'Belief in a creator is just wishful thinking.'
- 'Creation can only have a purpose if there was a creator.'
- 'Evidence supporting the existence of a creator is weak.'
- 'There is too much evidence around to argue that there is no creator.'
- 'Belief in a creator is as relevant today as it has always been.'
- 'The universe is meaningless.'
- 'There is little evidence that there is a creator.'
- 'Religion and science have opposing views on the creation of life.'
- 'Religion has clearly proved that there is a living creator in the universe.'

Statement question stems

- To what extent do you agree?
- How far do you agree?

- Is this statement fair?
- To what extent might scientists and religious people agree?
- How successfully can religious people support this view?
- To what extent might this view be supported?
- Analyse and evaluate this statement.
- Discuss.

Direct questions

- Is there enough evidence to support belief in a creator?
- To what extent do science and religion agree with the existence of a creator?
- To what extent can it be demonstrated that the universe does not require a creator?
- Why might some religious people and scientists agree on life having a creator?
- Discuss the strengths and weaknesses of belief in a creator.
- How successful have religious people been in using science to support belief in a creator?
- To what extent do religious people need science to prove the existence of a creator?
- How valid are scientific arguments against the existence of a creator?
- Why might some religious people disagree over the role a creator has played in creation?
- Have science and religion successfully shown that the existence of a creator is highly likely?

Issue: Distinction between literal and metaphorical interpretations of creation accounts

Angles

- Conflicting interpretations of creation accounts
- Understandings of creation accounts
- The purpose of creation accounts
- Science and creation accounts.

You need to know (describe):

- different religious views of creation accounts
- different non-religious views of creation accounts
- the content of creation accounts
- the purposes of creation accounts.

You need to be able to explain (analyse):

- the reasons for literal and metaphorical interpretations of creation accounts
- the symbolism found in creation accounts
- the ideas behind different understandings of creation accounts
- how creation accounts are used by religious people
- the reasons behind rejection of creation accounts
- the context of creation accounts.

You need to be able to comment on (evaluate):

- the strengths and weaknesses of religious and non-religious views of creation accounts
- the advantages and disadvantages of different ways of interpreting creation accounts
- the impact of modern discoveries of creation accounts
- the credibility of creation accounts today
- the implications of literal and metaphorical interpretations of creation accounts
- various issues identified by the questions (useless advice but true nonetheless).

You need to avoid:

- giving the impression that all religious people believe the same about creation accounts
- giving the impression that all scientists treat religion with contempt.

You need to look out for:

- questions that ask why religious people might disagree about interpreting creation stories.

Question approaches
Statements

- 'There is scientific support for religious creation accounts.'
- 'Belief in the literal truth of creation accounts is deluded.'
- 'Religious people cannot reject the creation accounts of their faith.'
- 'The only reasonable approach to religious creation accounts is to treat them as metaphorical.'
- 'Religious creation accounts have a greater symbolic than literal value.'
- 'Creation accounts still have some relevance today.'
- 'Science has little to contribute to understandings of religious creation accounts.'
- 'Creation accounts should be understood literally.'
- 'There is no need to completely reject religious creation accounts.'
- 'Religion has clearly shown that creation accounts have some value.'

Statement question stems

- To what extent do you agree?
- How far do you agree?
- Is this statement fair?
- To what extent might scientists and religious people agree?
- How successfully can religious people support this view?
- To what extent might this view be supported?
- Analyse and evaluate this statement.
- Discuss.

Direct questions

- Is there enough evidence to support literal understandings of creation accounts?
- To what extent do science and religion agree that creation accounts should not be read literally?
- To what extent can it be demonstrated that literal understandings of creation accounts are flawed?
- Why might some religious people accept a literal understanding of creation accounts?
- Discuss the strengths and weaknesses of a creation account you have studied.
- How successful have religious people been in defending their understandings of religious creation accounts?
- To what extent can religious creation accounts be disproved?
- How valid are arguments against a metaphorical understanding of religious creation accounts?
- Why might some religious people disagree about their understandings of religious creation accounts?
- To what extent do religious creation accounts support belief in a creator God?

Issue: Scientific theories: the Big Bang and evolution

Angles

- Big Bang and the role of a creator
- Evolution and the role of a creator
- Big Bang and creation accounts
- Evolution and creation accounts
- Scientific theories and belief.

You need to know (describe):

- key ideas of evolution and the Big Bang Theory
- ways in which religious people have used these ideas to support belief
- religious views on these theories
- current developments of the theories.

You need to be able to explain (analyse):

- the challenges to religious belief that are posed by these theories
- the reasons behind different religious rejection of the theories
- the reasons behind religious adoption of the theories
- the ways in which religious and scientific views of origins might be compatible.

You need to be able to comment on (evaluate):

- the strengths and weaknesses of Big Bang and evolution
- the impact of modern discoveries on beliefs about the nature of God
- the impact of modern discoveries on creation accounts

- the impact of modern discoveries on arguments supporting the existence of God
- various issues identified by the questions (useless advice but true nonetheless).

You need to avoid:

- giving the impression that all religious people believe the same about scientific views of the origins of life
- confusing the Big Bang with evolution.

You need to look out for:

- questions that specifically ask about the origins of the universe.

Question approaches
Statements

- 'Science can support the view that there is a creator.'
- 'Belief in a creator is just wishful thinking.'
- 'Evolution removes the need for belief in God.'
- 'Scientific evidence overwhelmingly proves that the origins of life were purely natural.'
- 'The Big Bang Theory is a completely satisfactory explanation for the origins of the universe.'
- 'If there is evolution there is no need for a creator.'
- 'In the light of scientific discoveries about the origins of life nobody should seriously believe creation stories.'
- 'Science has shown there is little evidence that there is a creator.'
- 'You cannot be religious and believe scientific accounts of origins.'
- 'Religion has clearly proved that God created the universe.'

Statement question stems

- To what extent do you agree?
- How far do you agree?
- Is this statement fair?
- To what extent might scientists and religious people agree?
- How successfully can religious people support this view?
- To what extent might this view be supported?
- Analyse and evaluate this statement.
- Discuss.

Direct questions

- Is there enough evidence to support religious views on the origins of life?
- To what extent do religious and scientific understandings of the universe suggest that it has a creator?
- To what extent can it be demonstrated that the universe does not require a creator?
- Discuss why some religious people believe that scientific explanations of the universe are inadequate.

- How convincing is the evidence that life appeared as a result of an intervention by a creator?
- How successful have religious people been in using science to support the belief that God is responsible for the origin of life?
- To what extent does science support religious beliefs about the origins of life?
- Why do some people consider that scientific discoveries have replaced religious explanations for the origins of life?
- Why might some religious people disagree over the role a creator has played in creation?
- To what extent are both science and religion needed to explain the origins of life?

Issue: Perspectives on the compatibility between reason and faith

Angles

- Conflict between reason and faith
- Relationship between reason and faith
- Compatibility of science and religious views of creation
- Sources of knowledge for faith and reason.

What you are likely to find here is that reason and faith issues are, in fact, discussed throughout your work on this unit. You will find that any time you are comparing science with religion you are actually reflecting on the compatibility between faith and reason. Your teacher will have given you examples of how religion and science disagree (this is where faith and reason are not compatible) and examples of where there is a mutual respect, understanding and sharing of ideas. The main point of this part of the course is to show that religious and non-religious people are not always at each other's throats and that there is much dialogue taking place between them.

You need to know (describe):

- different religious views of how the universe began
- why religious people hold different views on the origins of the universe
- the ways in which religious people use the sacred texts/science to explain origins
- reasons for religious agreement/disagreement on the origins of the universe
- how religious people make the Big Bang Theory fit into their beliefs
- why religious people see the Big Bang as proving the cosmological argument
- what reason is
- what faith is.

You need to avoid:

- giving the impression that all religious people believe the same about the origins of the universe
- mixing up different religious views.

You need to look out for:

- questions that focus just on reason
- questions that focus just on faith.

Question approaches
Statements

- 'Science can support the view that there is a creator.'
- 'Belief in a creator is just wishful thinking.'
- 'Creation can only have a purpose if there was a creator.'
- 'Evidence supporting the existence of a creator is weak.'
- 'There is too much evidence around to argue that there is no creator.'
- 'Belief in a creator is as relevant today as it has always been.'
- 'The universe is meaningless.'
- 'There is little evidence that there is a creator.'
- 'Religion and science have opposing views on the creation of life.'
- 'Religion has clearly proved that there is a living creator in the universe.'

Statement question stems

- To what extent do you agree?
- How far do you agree?
- Is this statement fair?
- To what extent might scientists and religious people agree?
- How successfully can religious people support this view?
- To what extent might this view be supported?
- Analyse and evaluate this statement.
- Discuss.

Direct questions

- Is there enough evidence to support belief in a creator?
- To what extent do science and religion agree with the existence of a creator?
- To what extent can it be demonstrated that the universe does not require a creator?
- Why might some religious people and scientists agree on life having a creator?
- Discuss the strengths and weaknesses of belief in a creator.
- How successful have religious people been in using science to support belief in a creator?
- To what extent do religious people need science to prove the existence of a creator?
- How valid are scientific arguments against the existence of a creator?
- Why might some religious people disagree over the role a creator has played in creation?
- Have science and religion successfully shown that the existence of a creator is highly likely?

Exemplar analysis and evaluation points: analysis and evaluation combined

> **Q** 'Evolutionary theory has removed the need for a designer of the universe.' Discuss.

The Good

This is a controversial statement. Christians have been quite successful in responding to it. There are three main groups of Christians and their responses to this challenge are different. The first thing I need to explain is what the challenge is. This statement is saying that the universe is all down to a mix of luck and natural laws. This means that the universe does not have a purpose. The literalist group of Christians see this as a challenge to their beliefs because they believe that God did design the universe and that he designed it in the way the Bible describes. Their response to the challenge is to say that evolution did not happen. This is a weak response because the evidence for evolution is so great that there is a good chance that it is a fact. It could be a strong response because they could argue that evolution is not a scientific fact yet – it is still a theory.

> Clear explanation of the question and the issue. Woohoo!

> A wee drop of analysis.

> And whoop, whoop, some evaluation. Spot on.

The second group of Christians are Intelligent Design Christians. Their scientists at the Discovery Institute say that evolution is natural but that God fine-tuned it to produce life like ours. They say that something as complex as the universe could not be the result of pure chance. This is a successful response because it uses scientific discoveries and does not make itself look stupid by saying that all evolution is wrong. It could be a weak response because it is trying to mix science and religion and use the God of the Gaps to explain things science cannot explain.

> Exact same process again. This is how you do it. Keep the structure simple.

The Bad

Christians are not successful in answering this challenge. They think that God designed the universe and that he made it like it says in the Bible. This is a bad idea because why does God allow people to suffer in evolution. Christians do not accept that some things might not need to be designed. It could be that we just like to think the universe is designed to make us feel a bit better rather than it all being luck. If Christians said that evolution was used by God to make the universe then maybe people would listen to them more and they could respond successfully to the challenge. Some Christians do believe evolution and say that the Bible is just a myth. This is a successful response because it shows that some Christians will listen to what science says and this will make them more modern and acceptable.

The first thing to notice is that there is a generalisation and this is often a sign that the candidate does not have a full grasp of what the issue is about. The second thing is that there is no structure. It is difficult to follow the candidate's line of thought. The candidate does make a couple of good points but because there is no structure these points are wasted.

The Ugly

I think that evolution proves that there is no designer. Evolution shows that things can change in small ways over time and that they only appear to be designed when they are not. There is no proof that there is a god or a designer and evolution shows this is true. Richard Dawkins says 'Truth is scientific truth' and Albert Einstein said 'Religion without science is lame and science without religion is blind.' This shows that there is no Designer because there is no proof.

This is dire. It is unlikely that the candidate would score any marks if the essay continued in this vein. The candidate has also given a personal view which is fine but it is not backed up by any reasoning. And another thing ... many candidates have done this over the years: the 'no proof of God's existence' statement. Try to avoid writing that. It is wrong, there is proof of the existence of God which some people accept and some people do not accept. If there was 'no proof' then we could not even have the debate. In any case using phrases like 'no proof' makes the answer sound like a bit of a rant.

The Existence of God

SQA Course Assessment Specification

Section 3: Religious and Philosophical Questions

The content in each Part describes ideas and arguments which may feature in both religious and non-religious responses.

Part B: The Existence of God

- The cosmological and teleological arguments
- Responses to the cosmological and teleological arguments
- The problem of evil
- Perspectives on the compatibility between reason and faith.

Issue: The cosmological argument and responses

Angles

- Science and the cosmological argument
- Philosophy and the cosmological argument
- Theology and the cosmological argument
- Evidence and the cosmological argument
- Strengths and weaknesses of the argument.

You need to know (describe):

- the cosmological argument and its developments
- the nature of god in the religious perspective from which you have studied the argument.

You need to be able to explain (analyse):

- the principles behind the argument
- the principles behind objections to the argument
- the ideas behind different understandings of the argument
- the ideas behind different religious views on how God's existence may be proved by the cosmological argument

- the reasons behind religious and non-religious criticisms of ideas relating to the argument
- similarities and differences between religious and non-religious views on the argument
- the implications of religious and non-religious views on the argument.

You need to be able to comment on (evaluate):

- the strengths and weaknesses of religious and non-religious views on the argument
- whether or not the argument can go further than proving the existence of a First Cause
- the relevance of religious and non-religious views on the argument
- various issues identified by the questions (useless advice but true nonetheless).

You need to avoid:

- giving the impression that all religious people believe the same about the argument
- agonising over your own personal view – often painful to read and exams are not the place to do it!
- giving the impression that science and religion are always in conflict
- claiming there is 'no proof' of God's existence. There is; it's just that some people think it is poor.

You need to look out for:

- mixing up teleological and cosmological – could be a very expensive mistake.

Question approaches
Statements

- 'Science has finally disproved the cosmological argument.'
- 'Science proves that the cosmological argument is right.'
- 'The cosmological argument fails as a philosophical argument.'
- 'The cosmological argument proves that there is a personal god behind the origins of the universe.'
- 'The cosmological argument can demonstrate that there was a First Cause, but nothing about the nature of the First Cause.'
- 'The cosmological argument fails to prove the existence of God.'
- 'The cosmological argument proves beyond all doubt that God exists.'
- 'The cosmological argument proves there is a First Cause and nothing else.'
- 'Objections do not succeed in undermining the cosmological argument.'
- 'Philosophical objections alone are enough to disprove the cosmological argument.'

Statement question stems

- To what extent do you agree?
- How far do you agree?
- Is this statement fair?
- To what extent might non-religious and religious people agree?
- How successfully can religious people support this view?

- To what extent might this view be supported?
- Analyse and evaluate this statement.
- Discuss.

Direct questions

- Why might some people argue that science disproves the existence of God?
- To what extent would religious people agree that the Big Bang supports arguments for a divine First Cause?
- Does there need to be a First Cause?
- Discuss the weaknesses of the First Cause argument.
- How convincing is the First Cause argument?
- How can it be argued that the First Cause argument is wrong?
- To what extent can the cosmological argument be successfully defended?

Issue: The teleological argument and responses

Angles

- Science and the teleological argument
- Philosophy and the teleological argument
- Theology and the teleological argument
- Evidence and the teleological argument
- Strengths and weaknesses of the argument.

You need to know (describe):

- the teleological argument and its developments
- the nature of god in the religious perspective from which you have studied the argument.

You need to be able to explain (analyse):

- the principles behind the argument
- the principles behind objections to the argument
- the ideas behind different understandings of the argument
- the ideas behind different religious views on how God's existence may be proved by the teleological argument
- the reasons behind religious and non-religious criticisms of ideas relating to the argument
- similarities and differences between religious and non-religious views on the argument
- the implications of religious and non-religious views on the argument.

You need to be able to comment on (evaluate):

- the strengths and weaknesses of religious and non-religious views on the argument
- whether or not the argument can go further than proving the existence of a First Cause
- the relevance of religious and non-religious views on the argument
- various issues identified by the questions (useless advice but true nonetheless).

You need to avoid:

- giving the impression that all religious people believe the same about the argument
- agonising over your own personal view – often painful to read and exams are not the place to do it!
- giving the impression that science and religion are always in conflict
- claiming there is 'no proof' of God's existence. There is; it's just that some people think it is poor.

You need to look out for:

- mixing up teleological and cosmological – could be a very expensive mistake.

Question approaches
Statements

- 'The design argument fails to prove the existence of God.'
- 'The teleological argument proves beyond all doubt that God exists.'
- 'The design argument proves nothing more than the possibility of a designer.'
- 'We choose to see design where there is none. Everything is down to a combination of natural laws and chance.'
- 'The teleological argument's main failure is the assumptions it makes.'
- 'Scientific discoveries make the existence of a designer more likely.'
- 'The teleological argument is more convincing than the cosmological argument.'
- 'The universe is exactly what we would expect it to be like if there was a designer.'
- 'The universe is exactly what we would expect it to be like if there was no designer.'
- 'It is more reasonable to believe that there is a designer than there is not a designer.'
- 'The arguments of science and religion about the presence of design in the universe are not as far apart as they think.'

Statement question stems

- To what extent do you agree?
- How far do you agree?
- Is this statement fair?
- To what extent might scientists and religious people agree?
- How successfully can religious people support this view?
- To what extent might this view be supported?
- Analyse and evaluate this statement.
- Discuss.

Direct questions

- Is the universe designed?
- Why do supporters of the design argument think that the universe requires a designer?
- Does the universe need a designer?
- How convincing is the design argument?

- How can it be argued that the teleological argument is wrong?
- Is the teleological argument more convincing than the cosmological argument?
- To what extent do arguments for the existence of God prove that his existence is highly likely?
- How successful are the criticisms of the design argument?
- Would it be fair to say that critics of the design argument have won the debate?
- Evaluate the teleological argument.

Issue: The problem of suffering and evil

Angles

- Evil as evidence of the non-existence of God
- Evil as evidence against the existence of a First Cause or designer
- Religious explanations of evil
- Philosophical explanations of evil
- Non-religious explanations of evil.

You need to know (describe):

- the nature of God
- the role of suffering in religious teaching
- religious and non-religious explanations of suffering.

You need to be able to explain (analyse):

- the challenges to belief in God that are posed by suffering
- the reasons behind different religious views of suffering
- the reasons behind non-religious views of suffering
- the ways in which religious and scientific views of suffering might be compatible.

You need to be able to comment on (evaluate):

- the strengths and weaknesses of suffering as evidence of the non-existence of God
- the impact of suffering on belief in God
- the impact of modern explanations of suffering on religion
- the strengths and weaknesses of religious explanations of suffering
- various issues identified by the questions (useless advice but true nonetheless).

You need to avoid:

- saying that God is a pure bam because he allows suffering
- going off on a tangent into the teleological argument since the two are quite closely linked.

You need to look out for:

- questions that specifically ask about the extent to which suffering is a problem for arguments in favour of the existence of God.

Question approaches
Statements

- 'The existence of suffering and evil show that the universe was neither created nor designed.'
- 'Belief in God is just wishful thinking.'
- 'Religious explanations of the existence of suffering and evil are inadequate.'
- 'The existence of suffering and evil is irrelevant in the debate about the First Cause/ design of the universe.'
- 'The problem of suffering and evil can be used to prove the existence of God.'
- 'Suffering and evil tell us more about human nature than they do about the existence of God.'
- 'Suffering and evil is not really a key issue in the debate about God's existence.'
- 'Suffering and evil highlight the need to change human understandings of God.'
- 'You cannot be religious and believe that God is responsible for suffering and evil.'
- 'Religion has clearly proved that in spite of all the issues, there is a God.'

Statement question stems

- To what extent do you agree?
- How far do you agree?
- Is this statement fair?
- To what extent might scientists and religious people agree?
- How successfully can religious people support this view?
- To what extent might this view be supported?
- Analyse and evaluate this statement.
- Discuss.

Direct questions

- Is there enough evidence to support religious views on responsibility of suffering and evil?
- To what extent do religious and non-religious understandings of the universe suggest suffering and evil is the responsibility of humanity?
- To what extent can it be demonstrated that God is responsible for suffering and evil?
- Discuss why some non-religious people believe that suffering and evil proves that there is no God.
- How convincing is the evidence that suffering and evil is proof that there is a God?
- How successful have non-religious people been in using suffering and evil as proof that there is no God?
- To what extent does religion succeed in overcoming the challenges posed by the existence of suffering and evil in relation to the existence of God?

- Why do some people consider that suffering and evil is not a problem for the existence of God?
- Why might some religious people disagree over the role suffering and evil has played in creation?
- To what extent are religious and non-religious views on suffering and evil weak?

Issue: Perspectives on the compatibility between reason and faith

Angles

- Conflict between reason and faith
- Relationship between reason and faith
- Compatibility of science and religious views of creation
- Sources of knowledge for faith and reason.

What you are likely to find here is that reason and faith issues are, in fact, discussed throughout your work on this unit. You will find that any time you are comparing non-religious views with religious views you are actually reflecting on the compatibility between faith and reason. Your teacher will have given you examples of how religious and non-religious views disagree (this is where faith and reason are not compatible) and examples of where there is a mutual respect, understanding and sharing of ideas. The main point of this part of the course is to show that religious and non-religious people are not always at each other's throats and that there is much dialogue taking place between them.

Exemplar analysis and evaluation points: analysis and evaluation combined

| Q | 'The existence of suffering and evil provides enough evidence to show that God does not exist.' Discuss. |

The Good

This idea is often used in arguments against the existence of God. It is not the strongest of arguments because all it is doing is proving that God does not have the characteristics he is claimed to have rather than disproving his existence. This essay will explain why some people argue that the existence of suffering and evil disproves God and then it will show why this is not a strong argument before going on to show that there are other reasons as to why God may not exist.

Clear point, but it has not been developed.

The first thing is that for Jews, Christians and Muslims, God is an all-loving, all-knowing, all-powerful good God. If God is all good then he will hate evil and want to get rid of it. If God is all-knowing then he will know how to get rid of it and if he is all-powerful then he can get rid of it. But, evil exists, so God cannot be all-powerful, all-knowing and all-loving.

Nice bit of analysis mixed with KU to set up the next point.

Some people use this as a reason to show that there is no God. It fails in many ways. They might argue that a good God would not allow evil to happen. There is no way that this can be supported. It is not logical for a start. Just as there are many good people in the world who allow evil to happen and sometimes even cause evil intentionally or unintentionally, it does not mean to say that they are not good. The same applies to God. Hitchens was very severe in his description of God's nature when imagining the prayers sent to God by the victims of Austrian child abuser, Hans Fritzl. Hitchens felt it was unbelievable that any God could sit by and watch that happen.

This paragraph has got the lot: KU, analysis, evaluation, sources, case studies. High quality.

This does not disprove the existence of God, all it does is question what God's role in creation is. God could be powerless and not be able to act or he could choose not to act because it would take interference too far or he may not be there or he may be completely indifferent in his attitude towards the universe. All of these are possibilities but Hitchens, and people like him, choose only one of these possibilities, i.e. there is evil, therefore God does not exist. That conclusion simply does not add up because it does not follow that evil conclusively proves that there is no God nor has there ever been. It may be used to prove what God is like but it cannot do any more than that. In fact it is a bit like the cosmological argument for God's existence – it does no more than offer proof that God might

Conclusion drawn – well done.

exist but it cannot say anything about what God might be like.

Another strong evaluative point. If the essay goes on like this, 20/20 is do-able.

The Bad

I think that the statement is right in what it says. If God is real then he would not let all the bad stuff happen in the world but he just sits back and lets it go on. I will show why suffering and evil proves that there is no way that there can be a God and then I will draw conclusions on the issue at the end of this essay.

This answer drifts in and out of making good points. What it lacks is detail. If the whole essay was done like this it would be one of those that would get around 9–11 out of 20, real touch and go stuff. Detailed argument is what is needed.

Christians believe that God is good and all powerful. If God is good he will want rid of evil and if God is all powerful then he will be able to get rid of evil. Evil exists so both of these statements about God cannot be true and if they cannot be true then God cannot exist. God is too full of contradictions to be real. God cannot create a boulder that is too heavy for him to lift so he cannot be both good and all powerful at the same time.

The Ugly

If God is real then he would not let all the bad stuff happen in the world. There is no way that there can be a God because of all of the bad stuff that goes on.

This is woeful. Some poor so-and-so has watched minutes of their precious life slip away as they read this. If the whole essay makes points as bad as this, RMPS teachers across the land will lose their sanity.

Christians believe that God is good and all powerful. God is too full of contradictions to be real. God cannot create a boulder that is too heavy for him to lift so he cannot be both good and all powerful at the same time.

The Problem of Evil and Suffering

SQA Course Assessment Specification

Section 3: Religious and Philosophical Questions

The content in each Part describes ideas and arguments which may feature in both religious and non-religious responses.

Part C: The Problem of Evil and Suffering
If God(s) is good, why do people suffer?

- Causes of evil and suffering
- Understandings of God(s) nature
- Freewill and responsibility
- Interpretations and responses to suffering
- Perspectives on the compatibility between reason and faith.

Issue: Causes of evil and suffering

Angles

- Challenge to God's nature arising from suffering and evil
- Nature of suffering and evil
- Religious and non-religious explanations of suffering and evil
- Role of suffering and evil in religion
- Role of suffering and evil in the world.

You need to know (describe):

- different religious views of the causes of suffering and evil
- different religious views on the role of God and suffering and evil
- different religious views on the purposes of suffering and evil
- different religious views on the origins of suffering and evil.

You need to be able to explain (analyse):

- the ideas behind different religious views of human nature (could use your World Religions notes for this)

- the ideas behind different understandings of the role of suffering and evil in religion
- the ideas behind different understandings of the role of suffering and evil from a non-religious perspective
- the challenges created for religion by the existence of suffering and evil
- similarities and differences between religious and non-religious views on suffering and evil
- the implications of religious and non-religious views on the role of suffering and evil in the universe
- strengths and weaknesses of beliefs about the causes of suffering and evil.

You need to be able to comment on (evaluate):

- the strengths and weaknesses of religious and non-religious views on the causes of suffering and evil
- how sound the religious and non-religious views are on the role of suffering and evil
- the relevance of religious and non-religious views on the causes of suffering and evil
- various issues identified by the questions (useless advice but true nonetheless).

You need to avoid:

- giving the impression that all religious people believe the same about suffering and evil
- giving the impression that religious and non-religious views are always in conflict
- arguing that a world without RMPS Higher exams would be a world without suffering and evil.

You need to look out for:

- questions that ask why religious people might disagree about the role and nature of suffering and evil.

Question approaches
Statements

- 'Suffering and evil is conclusive proof that there can be no God.'
- 'All suffering and evil is ultimately natural.'
- 'Suffering and evil has no ultimate purpose. They are just brute facts.'
- 'Religion must explain suffering and evil in the world before it can make claims about God's nature.'
- 'Religious explanations of natural and moral evil are inadequate.'
- 'Religious explanations of suffering and evil are intent on avoiding the obvious conclusion that they are God's fault.'
- 'Suffering and evil are the responsibility of humanity.'
- 'No explanations of suffering and evil can ever be adequate.'
- 'The existence of suffering and evil have no bearing on whether or not God exists.'
- 'Suffering and evil are not a problem for the universe; they are a requirement.'

Statement question stems

- To what extent do you agree?
- How far do you agree?
- Is this statement fair?
- To what extent might scientists and religious people agree?
- How successfully can religious people support this view?
- To what extent might this view be supported?
- Analyse and evaluate this statement.
- Discuss.

Direct questions

- Is suffering and evil enough to disprove the existence of God?
- To what extent do religious and non-religious people agree on the causes of suffering and evil?
- To what extent can it be demonstrated that the universe requires the existence of suffering and evil?
- Why might some religious people and non-religious people agree that the existence of suffering and evil cannot disprove the existence of God?
- Discuss the strengths and weaknesses of belief that suffering and evil is the responsibility of humanity.
- How successful have religious people been in using suffering and evil to prove the existence of God?
- To what extent do religious people need to explain the causes of suffering and evil?
- How valid are non-religious explanations of suffering and evil?
- Why might there be disagreement over religious explanations of the causes of suffering and evil?
- Have science and religion successfully shown that the existence of a creator is highly likely?

Issue: The nature of God

Angles

- Challenges to God's nature arising from suffering and evil
- Nature of God and the nature of suffering and evil
- Religious and non-religious explanations of suffering and evil
- Role of suffering and evil in religion
- Role of suffering and evil in the world.

You need to know (describe):

- different religious views of the causes of suffering and evil
- different understandings of God's nature
- different religious views on the role of God and suffering and evil

- different religious and non-religious views on the purposes of suffering and evil in relation to God
- different religious views on the origins of suffering and evil.

You need to be able to explain (analyse):

- the ideas behind different religious views of human nature (could use your World Religions notes for this)
- the ideas behind different understandings of the role of suffering and evil in religion
- the ideas behind different understandings of the role of suffering and evil from a non-religious perspective
- the challenges created for religion by the existence of suffering and evil
- similarities and differences between religious and non-religious views on suffering and evil
- the implications of religious and non-religion views on the role of suffering and evil in the universe
- strengths and weaknesses of beliefs about the causes of suffering and evil
- the impact of suffering and evil on beliefs about God/ultimate reality.

You need to be able to comment on (evaluate):

- the strengths and weaknesses of religious and non-religious views on religious explanations of God's role in suffering and evil
- how sound the religious and non-religious views are on the role of God in suffering and evil
- the relevance of religious and non-religious views on the role/nature of God and the existence of suffering and evil
- various issues identified by the questions (useless advice but true nonetheless).

You need to avoid:

- giving the impression that all religious people believe the same about suffering and evil
- giving the impression that religious and non-religious views are always in conflict
- getting angry at God for all the suffering and evil in the world; remember, he pulls the strings!

You need to look out for:

- questions that ask why religious people might disagree about the role of humanity/God in suffering and evil.

Question approaches
Statements

- 'Suffering and evil is conclusive proof that there can be no God.'
- 'All suffering and evil is God's responsibility.'
- 'Suffering and evil have ultimate purposes. They are part of God's plan.'

- 'Religion must explain suffering and evil in the world before it can make claims about God's nature.'
- 'Religious explanations of God's role in natural and moral evil are inadequate.'
- 'Religious explanations of suffering and evil are intent on avoiding the obvious conclusion that they are God's fault.'
- 'Suffering and evil are the responsibility of humanity.'
- 'No explanations of suffering and evil can ever be adequate.'
- 'The existence of suffering and evil have no bearing on whether or not God exists.'
- 'Suffering and evil are not a problem for the universe; they are a requirement.'

Statement question stems

- To what extent do you agree?
- How far do you agree?
- Is this statement fair?
- To what extent might scientists and religious people agree?
- How successfully can religious people support this view?
- To what extent might this view be supported?
- Analyse and evaluate this statement.
- Discuss.

Direct questions

- Is suffering and evil enough to disprove the existence of God?
- To what extent do religious and non-religious people agree on who has ultimate responsibility for suffering and evil?
- To what extent can it be demonstrated that the universe requires the existence of suffering and evil?
- Why might some religious people and non-religious people agree that the existence of suffering and evil cannot disprove the existence of God?
- Discuss the strengths and weaknesses of belief that suffering and evil is the responsibility of humanity.
- How successful have religious people been in using suffering and evil to prove the existence of God?
- To what extent do religious people need to explain the causes of suffering and evil?
- How valid are non-religious explanations of suffering and evil?
- Why might there be disagreement over religious explanations of the causes of suffering and evil?

Issue: Freewill and responsibility

Angles

- Challenges to God's nature arising from freewill
- Nature of God and freewill
- Religious and non-religious explanations of freewill and responsibility

- Role of freewill and responsibility in religion
- Role of freewill and responsibility in the world
- Role of freewill and responsibility in proving/disproving the existence of God.

You need to know (describe):

- different religious views of the causes of suffering and evil
- different understandings of God's nature
- different religious and non-religious views on freewill and responsibility
- different religious and non-religious views on the purposes of freewill.

You need to be able to explain (analyse):

- the ideas behind different religious views of human nature (could use your World Religions notes for this)
- the ideas behind different understandings of the role of freewill in religion
- the ideas behind different understandings of freewill from a non-religious perspective
- the challenges created for religion by the existence of freewill
- similarities and differences between religious and non-religious views on freewill
- the implications of religious and non-religious views on the role of freewill
- strengths and weaknesses of beliefs about the role and purpose of freewill
- the impact of freewill on beliefs about God/ultimate reality.

You need to be able to comment on (evaluate):

- the strengths and weaknesses of religious and non-religious views on religious explanations of freewill as an explanation of evil
- how sound the religious and non-religious views are on the role of freewill in suffering and evil
- the relevance of religious and non-religious views on the role of freewill in the universe
- various issues identified by the questions (useless advice but true nonetheless).

You need to avoid:

- giving the impression that all religious people believe the same about freewill
- giving the impression that religious and non-religious views are always in conflict
- exercising your freewill and not contributing to the annual class present for your RMPS teacher.

You need to look out for:

- questions that ask why religious people might disagree about the role of freewill in suffering and evil.

Question approaches
Statements

- 'Freewill is conclusive proof that there is a God.'
- 'All suffering and evil is the result of the abuse of freewill.'
- 'Suffering and evil have ultimate purposes. They are part of God's plan.'
- 'Freewill gives us more reason to reject belief in God than the existence of suffering and evil.'
- 'Religious explanations of freewill's role in natural and moral evil are inadequate.'
- 'Religious explanations of suffering and evil are intent on avoiding the obvious conclusion that they are God's fault.'
- 'Suffering and evil are the responsibility of humanity.'
- 'No explanations of suffering and evil can ever be adequate.'
- 'The existence of suffering and evil have no bearing on whether or not God exists.'
- 'Suffering and evil are not a problem for the universe; they are a requirement.'

Statement question stems

- To what extent do you agree?
- How far do you agree?
- Is this statement fair?
- To what extent might scientists and religious people agree?
- How successfully can religious people support this view?
- To what extent might this view be supported?
- Analyse and evaluate this statement.
- Discuss.

Direct questions

- Is freewill enough to prove the existence of God?
- To what extent do religious and non-religious people agree on who has the ultimate responsibility for suffering and evil?
- To what extent can it be demonstrated that humanity possesses freewill?
- Why might some religious people and non-religious people agree that the existence of suffering and evil cannot disprove the existence of God?
- Discuss the strengths and weaknesses of the belief that suffering and evil is the responsibility of humanity.
- How successful have religious people been in using freewill to prove the existence of God?
- To what extent do religious people need to explain the causes of suffering and evil?
- How valid are non-religious explanations of suffering and evil?
- Why might there be disagreement over religious explanations of the causes of suffering and evil?

Issue: Interpretations and responses to suffering and evil; Perspectives on the compatibility of faith and reason

Angles

Don't be worrying too much about these two because of two things: (a) their content is very similar, (b) all the angles above pretty much cover all that can be done in these aspects of the course.

What you are likely to find here is that reason and faith issues are, in fact, discussed throughout your work on this unit. You will find that any time you are comparing non-religious views with religious views you are actually reflecting on the compatibility between faith and reason. Your teacher will have given you examples of how they disagree (this is where faith and reason are not compatible) and examples of where there is a mutual respect, understanding and sharing of ideas. The main point of this part of the course is to show that religious and non-religious people are not always at each other's throats and that there is much dialogue taking place between them.

Exemplar analysis and evaluation points: analysis and evaluation combined

A brief note about this exemplar. Yes, it is very much like the one in the 'Existence of God' and that is because both topics cover this area. I could have devised another essay but I have mittens to knit for this winter and it is October already.

> **Q** 'Suffering and evil challenges belief in a good God.'
> Discuss.

The Good

This idea is often used in arguments against belief in a good God. This essay will explain why some people argue that the existence of suffering and evil shows that God is not good and how some people show that the problem of suffering and evil is something that is necessary for belief in a good God.

Jews, Christians and Muslims believe God is an all-loving, all-knowing, all-powerful good God. If God is all good then he will hate evil and want to get rid of it. If God is all-knowing then he will know how to get rid of it and if he is all-powerful then he can get rid of it. But, evil exists, so God cannot be all-powerful, all-knowing, all-loving.

Nice bit of analysis mixed with KU to set up the next point.

177

Some people use this as a reason to show that god is not good. It fails in many ways. They might argue that a good God would not allow evil to happen. There is no way that this can be supported. It is not logical for a start. Just as there are many good people in the world who allow evil to happen and sometimes even cause evil intentionally or unintentionally, it does not mean to say that they are not good. The same applies to God. Hitchens was very severe in his description of God's nature when imagining the prayers sent to God by the victims of Austrian child abuser, Hans Fritzl. Hitchens felt it was unbelievable that any God could sit by and watch that happen.

This paragraph has got the lot: KU, analysis, evaluation, sources, case studies. High quality.

This does not disprove the existence of God, all it does is question what God's role in creation is. God could be powerless and not be able to act or he could choose not to act because it would take interference too far or he may not be there or he may be completely indifferent in his attitude towards the universe. All of these are possibilities but Hitchens, and people like him, choose only one of these possibilities, i.e. there is evil, therefore God does not exist. That conclusion simply does not add up because it does not follow that evil conclusively proves that there is no God nor has there ever been. It may be used to prove what God is like but it cannot do any more than that. In fact it is a bit like the cosmological argument for God's existence- it does no more than offer proof that God might exist but it cannot say anything about what God might be like.

Conclusion drawn – well done.

Another strong evaluative point. If the essay goes on like this, 20/20 is do-able.

The Bad

I think that the statement is right in what it says. If God is real then he would not let all the bad stuff happen in the world but he just sits back and lets it go on. I will show why suffering and evil proves that there is no way that there can be a God and then I will draw conclusions on the issue at the end of this essay.

This answer drifts in and out of making good points. What it lacks is detail. If the whole essay was done like this it would be one of those that would get around 9–11 out of 20, real touch and go stuff. Detailed argument is what is needed.

Christians believe that God is good and all powerful. If God is good he will want rid of evil and if God is all powerful then he will be able to get rid of evil. Evil exists so both of these statements about God cannot be true and if they cannot be true then God cannot exist. God is too full of contradictions to be real. God cannot create a boulder that is too heavy for him to lift so he cannot be both good and all powerful at the same time.

The Ugly

If God is real then he would not let all the bad stuff happen in the world. There is no way that there can be a God because of all of the bad stuff that goes on.

This is woeful. Some poor so-and-so has to watch minutes of their precious life slip away as they read this. If the whole essay makes points as bad as this RMPS teachers across the land will lose their sanity.

Christians believe that God is good and all powerful. God is too full of contradictions to be real. God cannot create a boulder that is too heavy for him to lift so he cannot be both good and all powerful at the same time.

Internal assessments

Internal assessment is a vital part of the course. The SQA has a list of assessment standards for each unit. You have to provide evidence that you have met these standards during the course. How this is done is up to your teacher. A variety of evidence might be drawn from things like:

- Homework
- Formal class tests
- Discussions
- Powerpoints
- Presentations
- Prelims.

The teacher can get the evidence from more than one source. Teachers have a hard job here because they want to give you practice at writing essays but at the same time they do not want to wear you down with loads of tests. It is a difficult balance to achieve. It is important therefore that you make sure that all of the work you do is top quality because any part of it can be used as evidence to show you have attained Higher standard. If the evidence is not produced then an A Grade is never going to happen.

An explanation of what the SQA is looking for might be useful:

World Religion	
Outcome 1 The learner will: **1 Apply knowledge and understanding of the impact and significance of religion today, by:** 1.1 Explaining the meaning of a source related to a world religion today, in depth and with reference to relevant abstract ideas. 1.2 Interpreting possible implications of the source's meaning for the lives of followers, in depth and with reference to relevant abstract ideas. 1.3 Explaining one key belief and one key practice related to the source, in depth and with reference to relevant abstract ideas. 1.4 Explaining how the source informs the belief and practice, in depth and with reference to relevant abstract ideas. 1.5 Providing an in-depth comment on the significance of a religious belief, practice and source to people's lives today, with reference to different possible implications of the source.	This outcome is unlike the other two outcomes in that it is very different from what you are expected to do in the exam. Here you examine a source which explains something about a religious belief and practice. In most cases the source will be from a sacred book but it need not be. It is your teacher's shout. Basically, you have to explain what a source means and how it ties in with a belief and a practice you have studied. Best thing to do is explain how it is related and then give some depth to the explanation by explaining how the beliefs and practices work in real life. You need to explain how they affect the lives of followers and why they are important to some of the followers of the religion. A lot to get out of one source and a bit of a pain that it is not the kind of thing you do in the exam with World Religions. Ho-hum.

Morality and Belief	
Outcome 1 The learner will: **1 Apply knowledge and understanding of contemporary moral questions and responses, by:** 1.1 Explaining a contemporary moral question, in depth and with reference to relevant theoretical or abstract ideas. 1.2 Explaining a religious and a non-religious response to the question, in depth and with reference to relevant theoretical or abstract ideas.	For this standard you have to explain why a particular issue is a moral issue and then you have to go on and explain both a religious and non-religious response to the issue. You need to make sure that you do this in some depth so it would be good practice to use the MESS strategy referred to in this book. You can add to the depth of the answer by referring to a couple of sources.
Outcome 2 The learner will: **2 Evaluate religious and non-religious responses to contemporary moral questions, by:** 2.1 Explaining one possible consequence of a religious and a non-religious response to a contemporary moral question, in depth and with reference to relevant theoretical or abstract ideas. 2.2 Explaining a key strength and a key weakness of a religious and a non-religious response to a contemporary moral question, in depth and with reference to relevant theoretical or abstract ideas. 2.3 Expressing a detailed, reasoned and well-structured viewpoint on the question, explaining supporting evidence and responding to contrasting viewpoints.	The second thing you have to do is discuss what the consequences might be of a particular viewpoint. Once again using the MESS technique should help ensure that you do that. You need to show too that you are aware that viewpoints have both strengths and weaknesses. These have to be clearly explained before you give some overall viewpoint on the question you have answered where you have backed up what you have said with some reasons. Try to ensure that you keep your work tightly structured so the teacher can easily see where you are making your points.

Religious and Philosophical Questions	
Outcome 1 The learner will: **1 Apply knowledge and understanding of religious and philosophical questions, by:** 1.1 Explaining a religious and philosophical question, in depth and with reference to relevant theoretical or abstract ideas. 1.2 Explaining the significance of the question to people's lives, in depth.	This is an awkward wee standard because of the phrasing of the language but it is essentially saying that you should be able to explain what the question is about and have a clear idea about why the question is one that is debated in S6 Common Rooms and night club queues across this kingdom.
Outcome 2 The learner will: **2 Critically analyse a religious and philosophical question and responses, by:** 2.1 Explaining a religious response and a non-religious response to the question, in depth and with reference to relevant theoretical or abstract ideas. 2.2 Comparing the two responses, in depth and with reference to relevant theoretical or abstract ideas. 2.3 Presenting a detailed, reasoned and well-structured conclusion on the question and responses, explaining supporting evidence and responding to contrasting viewpoints.	The second outcome is a bit easier to follow. In this one you are just looking at religious and non-religious responses and doing a comparison of them. The comparison needs to be detailed so make sure you bring in various other ideas and show how the whole thing is all joined up. You have to give some overall viewpoint on the question you have answered where you have backed up what you have said with some reasons. Try to ensure that you keep your work tightly structured so the teacher can easily see where you are making your points.